IRISH STUDIES 5

ADVISORY EDITORS

Denis Egan, Oscott College, Birmingham; Barbara Hayley, St Patrick's College, Maynooth; John A. Jackson, Trinity College, Dublin; Patrick Keatinge, Trinity College, Dublin; John S. Kelly, Oxford University; Robert Kiely, Harvard University; Heinz Kosok, Wuppertal University; Emmet Larkin, University of Chicago; Oliver MacDonagh, Australian National University; Dermot McAleese, Trinity College, Dublin; Augustine Martin, University College, Dublin; M. A. G. Ó Tuathaigh, University College, Galway; David B. Wallace, University of Cambridge.

IRISH STUDIES 5

IRELAND AND BRITAIN SINCE 1922

EDITED BY P. J. DRUDY
TRINITY COLLEGE, DUBLIN

CAMBRIDGE UNIVERSITY PRESS

CAMBRIDGE
LONDON NEW YORK NEW ROCHELLE
MELBOURNE SYDNEY

Published by the Press Syndicate of the University of Cambridge
The Pitt Building, Trumpington Street, Cambridge CB2 1RP
32 East 57th Street, New York, NY 10022, USA
10 Stamford Road, Oakleigh, Melbourne 3166, Australia

© Cambridge University Press 1986

First published 1986

Printed in Great Britain at The Bath Press, Avon

British Library Cataloguing in Publication Data
Ireland and Britain since 1922.—(Irish studies, ISSN 0260–8480; 5)
1. Great Britain—Foreign relations—Ireland 2. Ireland—Foreign relations—Great Britain
I. Drudy, P. J. II. Series
327.410417   DA47.9.I73

ISBN 0-521-33209-5

Contents

		Page
	Preface	vii
1.	Ireland and Britain under the Union, 1800–1921: an overview M. A. G. Ó TUATHAIGH	1
2.	Britain and Irish constitutional development BASIL CHUBB	21
3.	Britain's legacy: government and administration RONAN FANNING	45
4.	Britain's legacy to the Irish social security system GEOFFREY COOK	65
5.	Anglo-Irish economic interdependence: from excessive intimacy to a wider embrace DERMOT McALEESE	87
6.	Migration between Ireland and Britain since Independence P. J. DRUDY	107
7.	The Irish in Britain JOHN A. JACKSON	125
8.	Unequal sovereigns: the diplomatic dimension of Anglo-Irish relations PATRICK KEATINGE	139
9.	Northern Ireland: the 'unfinished business' of Anglo-Irish relations PAUL ARTHUR	161
	Index	179

Preface

This is the fifth and final volume of an inter-disciplinary Irish Studies series published by Cambridge University Press. The aim of the series has been to bring together the research of the best scholars working on Ireland and Ireland's relationship with the wider world. This volume examines the nature of the relationship between Ireland and Britain with special reference to the period since the new Irish state was founded in 1922. It commences with an historical overview, setting out the main strands of the relationship between the two countries from the Union up to Independence. The rest of the volume examines various aspects of Britain's 'legacy' to Ireland – constitutional, political, social and economic – and it analyses the changes which have taken place in Anglo-Irish relations in recent decades, with special reference to the problems of Northern Ireland. Unfortunately, I have had to be selective in my choice of topics due to space constraints; it is hoped however that what has been included will be of some interest.

I am again indebted to my Advisory Editors who have been unfailingly helpful. Trinity College has provided invaluable back-up service for this volume and indeed for the entire series. My special thanks to Orla Sheehan and Caroline Gillespie who typed many manuscripts with skill and patience. Cambridge University Press agreed to publish five volumes of essays on Ireland; the Press has accomplished this in a highly professional manner. In particular, my warmest thanks to Dennis Forbes, Jill Walden and Andrew Brown of the Press for their advice and unstinting support. Frances Fawkes also played a key role as sub-editor in the production of the last three volumes. My most obvious debt is, of course, to the contributors. To these and to many others who gave help and encouragement I offer my sincere thanks.

Trinity College, Dublin P.J.D.
May, 1986

1 · Ireland and Britain under the Union, 1800–1921: an overview

M. A. G. Ó TUATHAIGH

Nature, it may be said, decreed that there should be a special relationship between Ireland and Britain. But the nature of that relationship, and its changing course over the centuries, has been shaped by many forces, of individual and collective will and purpose as well as by the unintended and unforeseen play of historical accident and the force of circumstance.[1] Throughout the centuries of recorded history the traffic between the two islands – in people, commerce and ideas – has been rich and reciprocal, and, at different times and in different ways, at once enriching and problematic. As successive incursions of Norsemen and Normans worked upon and into the fabric of Celtic society in Ireland, the interplay of dynastic rivalries and alliances, of the links of trade and commerce, the changing arts and implements of warfare, the currents of cultural exchange (in art and architecture, language and literature, law, political ideas, methods of agriculture and other aspects of material culture) all combined to increase the intimacy and the complexity of British-Irish relations throughout the medieval centuries.

However, the decisive phases in the formal construction of British-Irish relations were: (1) the conquest and colonisation of Ireland by the centralising British state during the sixteenth and seventeenth centuries, (2) the constitutional incorporation of Ireland into the unitary British state in 1801, and (3) the settlements of 1920–22, which saw the emergence of an Irish national state (with dominion status) for twenty-six counties of Ireland, while the six north-eastern counties remained an integral part of the British state, though with a substantial measure of devolved government (or 'home rule') within the six-county unit of Northern Ireland.

The conquest of Ireland in the period between the Tudors and the Williamite settlement was a protracted, uneven, and complex event. At its close, however, the king's writ ran throughout the entire island of Ireland; an ascendancy, exclusively Protestant in religion and with title to most of the land of the country, was established as a new ruling class, and enjoyed a parliament of its own in Dublin, though one which in certain crucial respects was always subject to the control or influence of the government in London. The new Protestant ruling class comprised a substantial element of planters or colonists, who had either been settled by the Crown and its agents, or who had simply migrated to Ireland in the course of the sixteenth and especially the seventeenth centuries. The land which these planters were granted, bought or rented, was land which had been confiscated from earlier owners, and these in their turn had either emigrated, migrated or remained on in their native place but reduced in rank and status and power. Moreover, in the aftermath of the Reformation and the great convulsion of western Christendom in the sixteenth century, religious affiliation was the key factor in the process of conquest and colonisation in Ireland. The new ruling class (planter and 'conformed' native alike) was Protestant in religion and constituted a distinct religious and, in many other ways, cultural minority at the top of the social ladder throughout most of the country. The defeated majority – including its dispossessed leaders – was Catholic in religion. Only in Ulster were the new settlers of the seventeenth century sufficiently numerous to constitute a large and socially variegated community in their own right. In time, and naturally, there was considerable interaction between newcomers and natives.

It is important that we understand the purpose and outcome of this first British conquest of Ireland if we are to grasp the significance of the act of Union of 1801 and the historical forces which were at work in the re-shaping of British-Irish relations in 1920–22. The British state of the early modern period was a centralising state which was also in the process of gaining a vast global empire. So far as Ireland was concerned the primary concern of British monarchs and their advisers was with security – the security of the realm and the security of the empire. The manner in which Ireland was ruled, those who were to be entrusted with the responsibility for ruling Ireland, the precise relationship between the Dublin parliament, the Westminster parliament, and the Crown, all of these issues were, in the last analysis, considered within the context of the absolute need for British national security. The fact that a majority of the Irish remained Catholic, and that the grounds for disaffection and grievance remained fertile at different levels of this Catholic community in Ireland, added further to British concern with internal order in Ireland as part of an over-all system of imperial security. Understandably, this concern was heightened in time of war.

It was an acute crisis of confidence in the security of Ireland from an imperial perspective which finally led to the decision to abolish the Irish 'colonial' parliament in Dublin, and to incorporate Ireland into the unitary British state (the United Kingdom of Great Britain and Ireland) at the end of the eighteenth century. Two main forces combined to bring matters to a head. Firstly, the Irish Protestant ascendancy, influenced by the American independence struggle (the event itself and the ideas which inspired it), and by their own intermittently frustrating experience of subordination to the political interests dominant at Westminister, began to articulate a version of 'colonial nationalism'. That is to say, they began to claim that their rights – including the historic rights of their parliament under the Crown – were not being properly respected; that their interests (including their economic interests) were being disregarded or flouted, and that the time had come for them to regain full and unfettered control for the Irish parliament over the affairs of Ireland, subject only to the authority of the Crown. In time, as French ideas came to reinforce the American and British Whig ideological influences, a minority of Protestants (mostly Presbyterian) went further and began to demand an independent Irish republic.

The crux of all this was that opinion among the Protestant

'nationalists' and reformers was divided on the crucial question of where the majority Catholic population in Ireland fitted into these plans. Some – most notably the Society of United Irishmen in the 1790s – sought the abolition of all religious divisions and discrimination between Irishmen; others saw political and parliamentary reforms as applying only to the 'Protestant Irish nation'. The Catholics, for their part, also responded to the ideological forces at play, with different social groups adopting such key concepts as 'rights', 'liberties', 'representation', 'popular sovereignty' and 'democracy', and defining them within the context and terms of their own historical experience and their current social predicament. The result, given the particular configuration of economic difficulty and social tension, historical grievance and sectarian fervour, present in different parts of Ireland, produced a major crisis of internal order and of national security in the 1790s. Internal social conflict, with strong sectarian overtones in particular parts of the country, combined with the threat and on a number of occasions the actuality of invasion by expeditionary forces from republican and Napoleonic France to force the British government to a total re-appraisal of the framework of British-Irish relations. The crisis of imperial security and imperial interest required urgent solution. Already the colonies in America had been lost. The wars with France were making heavy demands on resources, notably military and naval resources. It was intolerable, therefore, that major resources should have to be diverted to quelling rebellion in Ireland, as had happened in 1798. Clearly, the local ascendancy in Ireland could no longer be relied upon to maintain internal security there; their political constancy, their collective nerve, and their basic competence to guarantee the security of Ireland within the Empire, were all now suspect. Accordingly, the British government decided to press ahead urgently with a solution to British-Irish relations which had been mooted some time earlier, namely a union of the two kingdoms (such as had already been made between England and Scotland in 1707), with one crown and one parliament at Westminster.

While immediate British intentions on the enactment of the Union are clear, the position is more confused when we turn to consider Irish responses to the proposal. The Protestant ascendancy – shaken by the violence of the 1798 rebellion – was divided in its calculation of individual, class, and national interest. Eventually – at the second asking – a majority of the Irish parliament voted for the Union proposals. The more vigorous Protestant opposition to the Union came from those (substantially Orangemen) who feared that the imperial parliament in Westminster would be less firm in its denial of further concessions to Catholics and in its defence of the Protestant ascendancy position in Ireland than the Dublin parliament had been.

The same assumption worked to a different effect on members of the Catholic hierarchy in Ireland. Alarmed at the spread of socially radical ideas (inspired by French revolutionary propaganda) among sections of the Irish masses; encouraged by the fact that most of the main concessions to Catholics in the previous twenty years had been made by the Irish Protestant parliament at the behest and insistence of the government in London; and reassured by Pitt and others that the removal of the remaining civil and political disabilities against Catholics (notably the oath which precluded them from entering parliament) would accompany or follow on the heels of the Union, the majority of the Irish Catholic bishops gave their support to the Union proposals. A section of the Catholic middle-class, led by the young lawyer Daniel O'Connell, opposed the Union on the grounds that it was a betrayal – and most likely an illegal act – by the Irish parliament of the historic national rights of the kingdom of Ireland. For the bulk of the Catholic masses – and especially the poorer classes – the demise of the old Irish parliament and the passing of the act of Union were largely matters of supreme indifference to them.

By the terms of the Union the Irish parliament was abolished, and from 1801 Ireland was to be represented in the parliament at Westminster by one hundred members of parliament in the

House of Commons, and twenty-eight Irish peers and four bishops in the House of Lords. The Established Churches of England and Ireland were united as the Established Church of England and Ireland. Ireland's financial contribution to the joint United Kingdom expenditure was set at two-seventeenths of the total, and after a short interval the exchequers and financial systems of the two countries were merged. Likewise in trade and commerce, after a short transition period customs and tariffs were removed and a single free trade area was created between the two islands.

The Union was a decisive moment in the history of British-Irish relations. But its significance was not quite the same for both partners. For Ireland the British connection was the dominant, ever-present reality in any contemplation of the country's predicament, problems or prospects. But Ireland only became a priority issue for British statesmen at particular moments of crisis – 1829, the mid-1840s, the late 1860s, the years of the Land War and of the Home Rule crisis of 1879–86, and again during 1912–22. Even during such crises Ireland was only one of a number of major issues pressing for the attention of imperial statesmen presiding over the most powerful global empire in the world. While successive Irish crises may have provided the occasion, and part of the cause, for the break-up of a number of British governments during the nineteenth century, it must be emphasised that Ireland was never given sustained attention as a top priority by any British government during the Union era.

This suggests further paradoxes in the operation of the Union. Though the Union made Ireland an integral part of the United Kingdom, nevertheless the presence in Dublin of a Viceroy and of a distinct administrative system more closely resembled the style of colonial government than that of 'another region' in the United Kingdom. Again, the fact that Irish circumstances and Irish problems required (and produced) a large body of 'exceptional' legislative measures and state interventions by successive British governments aptly illustrates that which was the dominant view of the British political establishment throughout the nineteenth century – that, whatever about the constitutional position, Ireland and the Irish experience were different from any other part of the United Kingdom in a number of crucial respects. Solutions to Irish problems need not necessarily, and in all probability would not, be based on the 'norms' operating in British society as a whole. Finding Irish solutions to Irish problems became part of the strategy of government pursued by various British cabinets during the second half of the nineteenth century.

Thus, for example, from the second quarter of the century Ireland had a centralised national police force and a centralised state system of elementary education – both without parallel in any other part of the United Kingdom at the time. Again, in the aftermath of the Famine, Irish conditions prompted a re-examination of the received wisdom (and theory) on land and political economy by some political economists and some influential political figures in Britain. The clearest acknowledgement of the particularity of Irish economic conditions and social attitudes came in the closing decades of the nineteenth and in the early years of the twentieth century – with direct state intervention (through a series of land acts) firstly in the regulation of rents and subsequently in the large-scale transfer of land-ownership in Ireland to those who occupied and farmed the land. Again, the establishment of the Congested Districts Board in 1891 (to generate economic and social improvements in the poorer areas of the western half of the country) was the first step towards addressing the problem of regional imbalance and economic retardation in any part of the then United Kingdom.

One might easily add further examples, but it is not necessary to labour the point. In many important respects Ireland was an 'exceptional' part of the United Kingdom throughout the period of the Union. Just how 'exceptional' was the point which nationalists of various kinds sought to make again and again in support of their claims for an Irish national state. So far as these claims were concerned, for republican separatists (from Tone to the Fenians and to the 1916 revolutionaries) the Union was merely a symbol of British domination of Ireland. For them the issue of Ireland's claim to national sovereignty was perfectly clear. As the 1916 Proclamation put it: 'We declare the right of the people of Ireland to the ownership of Ireland, and to the unfettered control of Irish destinies, to be sovereign and indefeasible.'

However, for constitutional nationalists, whether in the Repeal movement of the 1840s or the Home Rule movement later in the century, the terms of the Union were inevitably the point of departure in any demand for a redefinition of Ireland's constitutional status relative to Britain. In the case of O'Connell's claim for Repeal of the Union, the demand for an independent Irish kingdom linked with Britain by a common monarch was based on two principal grounds – historic legal rights, and the claim that Ireland was being misgoverned or badly governed under the Union, or, at the very least, was being governed less well than it would be under a native sovereign Irish parliament. The Home Rule case (though its demand for devolved government was decidedly less ambitious than the Repeal claim) used essentially the same arguments. In both instances popular support was mobilised through the harnessing of historic and contemporary grievances to the movement for political change. The identification of the Union arrangement as the source of Ireland's problems in the last century inevitably (and mistakenly) led many to the conclusion that the undoing of the same Union would act as some kind of panacea for these problems. The catastrophe of the Famine; the heavy emigration and consequent social dislocation which Ireland experienced from the 1830s but especially during the Famine and post-famine decades; the industrial retardation of most of the regions of Ireland (including Dublin's stagnation as a 'deposed capital' during the nineteenth century); the seemingly inexorable decline of the Irish language as a living language, and the general intensification of 'anglicisation' produced by state-sponsored elementary education, increased mobility and improved communications between Britain and Ireland, and the incentives to language change and cultural conformity provided by heavy Irish emigration to every corner of the English-speaking world; these and a host of other problems endured by Ireland during the nineteenth century were attributed by Irish nationalists (with varying degrees of consistency and indignation) to 'the connection with England' and in particular to the Union which defined and regulated that connection.

However, if the Union served as a focus for the collective sense of grievance, resentment and indignation of Irish nationalists (and it did so only when popular discontent was skilfully mobilised for political purposes by leaders such as O'Connell and Parnell), the Union was the focus for firm loyalty and support from those sections of Irish society who had either prospered under the Union or who perceived their present and future well-being and prosperity as being bound up with its maintenance. These elements included the wealthier Protestant bourgeoisie (commercial and professional) whose careers and export markets were defined in terms of the Empire. The Protestant landed ascendancy, with a few notable exceptions, retained a firm loyalty to the Union, notwithstanding the fact that throughout the nineteenth century their specifically religious privileges were dismantled, and their economic power based on landed property relentlessly whittled away by bad debts and bad management, rates and recessions, but most decisively by the 'Land War' of 1879–82 and the Land Acts which followed in the following twenty-five years. The eclipse of the specifically land-based power of the old ascendancy may be gauged from the fact that where in 1870 only a mere 3 per cent of the occupiers of farms in Ireland were owners of those farms, by 1920 some 65 per cent of those farmers were either owners already or on their way to purchasing their holdings. Of course, habits of mind and authority, ingrained attitudes of arrogance on the one hand and deference on the other, continued to operate for some time after the economic basis for such attitudes had begun to crumble. In the same way, the remnants of the landed ascendancy proved remarkably adept at maintaining social privileges bought by rank and title, well into the twentieth century in Ireland. But the Protestant Unionist tradition based on the big house – a tradition and a way of life which, in grandeur and decline, has inspired an extraordinary rich crop of literary works – was already in its twilight period in the generation before 1922. Its political Unionism, though generally firm, was no longer the aggressive edge of Irish Unionism.

This aggressive edge was, by the late nineteenth century at the latest, provided by the Ulster Unionists. The heavy regional concentration of aggressive Unionism in Ulster was, of course, due to many factors. This was the only region where the seventeeenth-century colonisation had succeeded in settling a large community of Protestant planters. Moreover, with the rapid growth of an enclave of industrial prosperity in Belfast and its hinterland – exploiting and requiring access to the far-flung markets of the British empire – this was the only region in Ireland which had clearly prospered under the Union. Accordingly, 'any advocate of constitutional changes in the relationship between Ireland and Britain who sought to enlist the support of the Protestants of the northeast would have to satisfy them that such changes would not (through tariff policy etc.) threaten the regional economy.'[2] No nationalist leader in the nineteenth century was able to so convince them.

But there was another dimension to Ulster Unionist determination besides the calculation of economic advantage. The Catholics were the majority in Ireland, and as the nineteenth century advanced this came to matter more and more. With the gradual extension of the franchise in the British state (from 1832 to 1918) the Catholics came to predominate in the electorate of the majority of constituencies in Ireland. With the reform of local government in 1898 Irish Catholics – longschooled in the business of political organisation and agitation since the days of O'Connell – began to actually assume positions of power and authority and local prestige in the business of the newly-established county councils. Furthermore, the strong cohesive sense of community which history, as it were, had bequeathed to Irish Catholics, was strengthened during the nineteenth century as an increasingly numerous and influential clerical establishment (bishops, priests, nuns and brothers) administered and ministered to a well-disciplined, strongly-conformist body of practising Catholics. The fact that the state system of elementary education had become, almost from its inception, effectively denominational, further reinforced community solidarity along religious lines. Finally, the Catholic hierarchy in Ireland at the end of the nineteenth century was not the cautious, apprehensive, concession-seeking body which had assured the government of its support at the time of the Union a century before. Its missionaries were going out to every corner of the globe; its emigrants were (even allowing for all the problems) the backbone of the Catholic communities throughout the English-speaking world (not least in Britain itself); its flock were overwhelmingly loyal and obedient to its authority; it was confident of its power and of its prestige.

This power and prestige, and how they might be exercised in an independent or 'Home Rule' Ireland caused nightmares for many Ulster (and not only Ulster) Protestants. Having themselves enjoyed, in varying degrees, the benefits of ascendancy and privilege for so long, the fear of losing such privileges as remained or of being faced with the establishment of a form of Catholic ascendancy in an Irish state was a powerful factor in stiffening the Ulster Unionist resistance to Home Rule in the period 1885–1920. The deeper passions of prejudice and fear had plenty of material from which to construct a rational statement of political intransigence.

The general elections of 1885–86 clearly indicated the geographic dimension of political division in Ireland. The Home Rule party won eighty-four of the one-hundred-and-three seats in Ireland. The Unionists' seats were almost entirely gained in the eastern half of Ulster, and overall representation in Ulster as a whole was evenly divided (and remained so down to the 1910 elections) between Nationalists and Unionists. The year 1885–86 was significant for another reason also. For the first time since the passing of the Union in

1800 a British prime minister, Gladstone, had committed himself and his party to altering the constitutional status of Ireland; in effect, to interfering with the Union. Whatever may have been Gladstone's reasons for advocating Home Rule for Ireland in late 1885, his decision was fateful for the future of British-Irish relations in the next forty years. It was clear from 1885–86 that sooner or later some form of devolved government would come to Ireland; that a particular problem would be encountered in trying to make such an arrangement acceptable to the concentrated Unionist minority in Ulster; and that the security of the Empire would remain a paramount condition for the concession of any form of self-government for Ireland. The precise mix of forces which exploded in Ireland between 1912 and 1922 could not, perhaps, have been predicted. But the essential problems which finally demanded solutions in 1920–22 were already clear forty years previously.

The Nationalist demand for some form of Irish national state drew its sustenance, as we have seen, from a variety of sources. While the historically-rooted sense of grievance of Irish Catholics was a powerful force when mobilised, Irish nationalism was never exclusively a Catholic idea. Indeed in the formulation of Irish nationalist ideology – and in particular in the search for an inclusive definition of Irish identity or nationality – Protestant writers and thinkers had been disproportionately numerous and influential (Tone, Davis, Parnell, Hyde and, in his way, Yeats). But the majority support which Irish nationalist movements enjoyed – from Repeal to Home Rule and thence to Sinn Féin in 1918 – needed to be mobilised on the issue of misgovernment or bad government; the charge that Ireland had not been fairly treated and had not done well under the Westminster parliament, and the further charge that Ireland could not expect fair treatment from a parliament where Irish interests were never the primary concern, a parliament which in times past had authorised the subjugation of Ireland and which held a major responsibility for its current economic retardation and social problems.

Those who attributed Ireland's economic difficulties in the nineteenth century to the effects of Union would have done well to ponder the implications of the fact that already *before* the Union came into operation Ireland's trade was massively dependent on Britain; by 1800 over 85 per cent of all Irish exports went to Britain, while almost 80 per cent of Irish imports came from Britain. They might also have considered the fact that the Union was passed at a moment in British economic history when she was already well into her take-off as the first industrial nation in the world. The spread of industrialisation was a geographically uneven process. The location of raw materials and markets, the pace of change in the technology of production and transport, the supply of quality entrepreneurs; the interplay of these and other factors produced profound and dramatic shifts in the relative power and prosperity of different states in Europe and of different regions within these states. Identifying the role played by state intervention in this process is a complex matter. But, as Horace Plunkett once remarked, in Ireland political economy was spelt with a capital 'p' and a small 'e'. Certainly there can be no doubting the fact that Irish nationalists in the Union period placed great trust and emphasis on the political status of Ireland in their analysis of what was wrong with the country and the steps that were needed to put things right.

It would be misleading, however, to claim that all manifestations of Irish nationalist sentiment during the Union period invariably or inevitably demanded a change in the constitutional relationship between Britain and Ireland. The different forms taken by Irish cultural nationalism is a case in point. A number of interesting cultural nationalists refused to accept that there was any inexorable political logic to their concern with the cultivation of Ireland's distinctive genius in such areas as language and literature. Sir Samuel Ferguson, for example, while firmly committed to the cultivation of an Irish national literature (in the English language but based on the rich Gaelic literary inheritance), and while frequently showing a familiar impatience with the insensitivity of English politicians to Irish realities, nevertheless remained convinced that the Union framework offered, on balance, the constitutional framework most conducive to individual liberty and the public good in Ireland.

Ferguson's position, like that of Sir Walter Scott and of some others sympathetic to the cultural dimension of national identity in Scotland and Wales, was a desire for cultural diversity or pluralism within the British state. In more recent times, those in Scotland and Wales (and to a much more limited extent in Northern Ireland) who combine such political unionism with a version of cultural nationalism, frequently concentrate on such areas as language, education and telecommunications as key areas within which cultural diversity must be carefully cultivated and promoted within the unitary British state. In the case of Northern Ireland's Unionists, however, the fact that cultural nationalism has been so closely linked with political nationalism in the mainstream of Irish nationalist writing during the past century and a half, has meant that a substantial body of Northern Unionists have deliberately cut themselves off from any contact with the older, indigenous culture of the land in which they live. The identity crisis which the political crisis of the past seventeen years has forced upon Northern Unionists has provoked some re-examination of attitudes towards the total cultural inheritance of the region. But political polarisation still exerts enormous pressure for cultural exclusivism among the two communities within the sharply divided society of Northern Ireland. Ferguson has found relatively few followers in his native eastern Ulster.

The dilemma of the cultural nationalist seeking to avoid or to ignore political entanglements is well-illustrated in the case of Douglas Hyde. Hyde, one of the founders of the Gaelic League, was a passionate believer in cultural nationalism. The necessity for Ireland, if she were to retain a distinct (and recognisable) national identity was, according to Hyde, that she de-anglicise herself, in language, customs, and habits of mind. Specifically, Hyde sought to keep the language revival movement (and the general cultural regeneration which he advocated) free from entanglement with any specific political programme, a 'broad church' for Irish patriots of every political persuasion. But Hyde failed in his endeavour. The majority, and certainly the most committed, of Hyde's followers were political separatists as well as cultural nationalists. Pearse put it bluntly when he announced that he and others of like mind had seen their Gaelic League evangelising as part of a larger enterprise of national liberation, a necessary exercise in consciousness-raising to prepare the way for political freedom. At the Gaelic League Árd Fheis of 1915 Hyde saw his version of a kind of apolitical cultural nationalism rejected by the majority, and the language movement inextricably linked to the struggle for political independence.

Hyde should not have been surprised by the events of 1915 in the Gaelic League. Because, in truth, cultural nationalism of an apolitical or indeed of an implicitly Unionist variety was always a minority view in nineteenth-century Ireland. The dominant view among those who espoused versions of cultural nationalism (e.g. the Young Irelanders, some of the Fenians, the Gaelic Athletic Association, D.P. Moran's Irish-Ireland movement, Sinn Féin and Hyde's own Gaelic League) was that, just as the cultural and economic subordination of Ireland had followed the loss of its political independence in the sixteenth and seventeenth centuries, so also the restoration of political independence would be a prerequisite for the reversal of the processes of cultural assimilation and economic dependence. This view of political independence, as the key determinant of cultural renewal and social and economic progress, was to have crucial bearing on the development of the independent Irish state in the first forty years after the establishment of Saorstát Éireann in 1922. It influenced ideas which shaped economic policy, in particular the economic nationalism which underlay Fianna Fáil's protectionist strategy from the 1930s to the late 1950s. It influenced the intention and the precise form of state intervention in areas such as education, censorship, and social legislation. Stated simply, it was assumed that an Irish state, under independent Irish control, could and would devise policies designed to erase the colonial attitudes of deference and dependence, and that it could create the climate (legislative, moral and intellectual) for the formation of an 'independent Irish mind', and for the enjoyment of a 'national life of its own' by Ireland. This was a large assumption, even if we allow that some of the statesmen and thinkers at the foundation of the Irish state had a more subtle grasp than others of the drastic complexity of its implications.

With the benefit of hindsight we can now see that there was considerable naiveté in this very exalted view of the creative possibilities of political sovereignty. In terms of economic development, for example, the fact that, to all intents and purposes, a single market area for the free flow of capital and labour continued to exist between Ireland and Britain in the half-century after 1922, may seem odd in the light of the rhetoric of economic nationalism inherited from the old Sinn Féin movement. In reality, of course, full-blooded economic nationalism was not a policy pursued by any Irish government since 1922. Even the first Fianna Fáil government of De Valera in 1932, undoubtedly the administration most committed to the *ideas* of economic nationalism, only persisted with a thorough-going protectionist policy aimed at economic self-sufficiency for a brief interval in the mid-1930s. By 1938 (in the Anglo-Irish treaty of that year) Fianna Fáil were already moving back from full-blooded self-sufficiency, and were, in fact acknowledging the fact that an abrupt break with the British market for Irish agricultural produce would produce serious social disruption and distress within the agricultural society in Ireland, unless 'good' (i.e. accessible and at reasonable cost) alternative markets could be found. As it happened, such alternative markets were not easily found, and even the availability since 1972 of the EEC outlet for Irish agricultural produce has not solved all the problems of Irish agriculture.

In the same way, the economic logic of geography and its implications for transport costs, dictated that Britain would continue to enjoy many advantages as a supplier of certain raw materials and finished goods for the Irish economy, no matter what the political or constitutional arrangements between the two islands. These lessons were learned over time. Defying or, at the least, seeking to blunt the economic implications of Ireland's geographical location relative to Britain would have demanded from a Dublin government policies far more radical than anything that either successive Dublin governments or their electorates would have considered acceptable. In short, no Dublin government between 1922 and 1972 (when Ireland joined the EEC) seriously considered making Ireland the Cuba, as it were, of the North Atlantic.

Again, if we turn for a moment to the question of cultural independence in the Irish state, we may state at once that the policy of 'de-anglicisation' was seriously advocated only by a section of the political leadership who wielded power in the state in the first generation after Independence, even if this minority included such key figures as De Valera, MacNeill, Blythe and Ó Ceallaigh. But it is clear that state policy for the revival of the Irish language seriously underestimated the difficulty and the complexity of the task of bringing about a major language change among the bulk of the population in an 'open' democratic society. The complex relationship between attitude and practice, the need for systematic planning, the link between language-learning at school and the use of that language in other spheres of life, the ideological context with which a successful language restoration/revival policy can be formulated – these and many other aspects of the language revival policy were only imperfectly or tardily understood, even by those most fervently committed to the policy of national cultural revival. Others found the equation of cultural renewal with language revival policy by government spokesmen too narrow; some came in time to resent and to reject entirely the official rhetoric. Others still – notably writers and intellectuals and ideologues – found that the real cultural battleground in post-independence Ireland was between the advocates of a substantially confessional state in conformity with the social and moral teaching of the Catholic church, and those who, from a republican, secular or libertarian point of view, demanded a more pluralist version of cultural growth. The tensions and confusions, contradictions and recriminations which marked the public debate on what exactly constituted 'Irish culture' (with its obsessive concern with essence and authenticity), indicated a deep sense of cultural insecurity and a lack of real cultural cohesion (apart from the strong bonding of the religious community) within the Irish national state in the early decades after Independence.

This may well be, as some commentators have suggested, a familiar and predictable condition for a post-colonial society. But it must also be acknowledged that, whatever the intentions or aspirations of nationalist leaders of the state since Independence, the real possibilities of disengagement from the dominant imperial culture have actually diminished in recent decades, as developments in telecommunications and the mass media have rendered almost entirely redundant notions of cultural 'protectionism' or even a state-led cultural selectivity from the increasingly de-regulated supply of ideas, information and entertainment through a variety of telecommunication networks. That American sources have come to dominate this Atlantic culture-flow is really beside the point: cultural hegemony is a natural corollary of economic dominance. What is incontestable, however, given Ireland's geographic location and linguistic circumstances, is that for any government in Ireland to attempt to exclude or even to drastically limit the dominant cultural influences of the powerful Anglo-American communications systems (assuming this to be technologically possible) would necessitate a degree of interference in individual liberties, private interests, and social habits of a kind which might not be easily accepted by the majority of the people in the state. This is the dilemma of many small, 'open', democratic states, anxious to maintain and develop their distinctive national cultures in a world where they are bombarded by media products emanating from a number of powerful sources outside their control. Ireland's predicament is not unique, though the fact that English is the main vernacular in the country greatly adds to its 'accessibility'.

We need go no further than these few examples of post-independence Irish experience to realise that they raise a number of serious questions about nationalist assumptions regarding the key role of constitutional arrangements in defining and explaining the complex nature of British-Irish relations. The period of the Union is undoubtedly a critical phase in the history of the relationship between the two islands and their peoples. But all that happened in Ireland and to Ireland, for good or ill, under the Union cannot be attributed to or explained by that Union operating as a system of government for the two countries. As we have seen, Ireland's economic dependence upon (or integration into) the British economy was already a fact before the Union was enacted. Likewise, the dominant partner had exercised a significant measure of cultural hegemony (e.g. in language and laws, though not in religion) for several centuries before the Union.

Irish nationalists of the nineteenth century may have attributed too much to constitutional status as the key determinant of social, cultural and economic development within Ireland itself. They may have used the Union from time to time as a kind of 'diabolus ex machina' to explain all the manifold problems of their own society. This is not to suggest that they were wrong to demand political independence for their country, or that political independence does not prove the most desirable and potentially the most fruitful setting within which any people sharing a common sense of national identity can develop and improve itself and make its mark among the community of nations. However, the experience of Ireland, and the course of British-Irish relations since 1922, suggest that formal political independence does not *in itself* guarantee success in achieving that 'independent national life' to which most anti-colonial liberation movements are dedicated. The process of de-colonisation is not simply an exercise in erasing, expunging and substituting. As many new post-colonial states have discovered in this century, the achievement of political-constitutional independence is the beginning and not the end of the task of national liberation.

These new states may learn valuable lessons from the Irish experience, under the Union and since Independence. So too may the Irish themselves.

REFERENCES

1. As the main historical data used in this essay are readily accessible in the standard historical surveys of the period, we will confine ourselves here to mentioning a number of special studies of British-Irish relations whose interpretations are particularly original, provocative or elegant – and in some instances all three. The short list must include Patrick O'Farrell, *Ireland's English Question: Anglo-Irish Relations 1534–1970* (London, 1971) and *England and Ireland since 1800* (Oxford, 1975); Oliver MacDonagh, *Ireland* (New Jersey, 1968) and *States of Mind: A Study of Anglo-Irish Conflict 1780–1980* (London, 1983); Nicholas Mansergh, *The Irish Question 1840–1921* (London, 1965); D. George Boyce, *Nationalism in Ireland* (London and Dublin, 1982); Tom Garvin, *The Evolution of Irish Nationalist Politics* (Dublin, 1981); F. S. L. Lyons, *Culture and Anarchy in Ireland 1890–1939* (Oxford, 1979).
2. Gearóid Ó Tuathaigh, *Ireland before the Famine, 1798–1848* (Dublin, 1972), p. 39.

2 · Britain and Irish constitutional development

BASIL CHUBB

Irish government today is carried on within the framework laid down in a Constitution, Bunreacht na hÉireann, that dates from 1937. That Constitution is the successor of two previous constitutions, the Constitution of the Irish Free State (1922) and the Constitution of Dáil Éireann (1919) which was created by Sinn Féin as part of the political struggle for independence. All three are best viewed as the products of a process of emancipation from British domination and emergence from the British political system. They were milestones in the evolution of the country's relationship with the United Kingdom and marked stages in the transition from a province of an essentially English state to a sovereign republic.

Likewise, much of the constitutional development that took place principally by way of amendment and judicial interpretation of the Constitutions themselves and by ordinary legislation can be viewed in the same light, at least until recently. Since the early 1970s, however, Ireland's membership of the European Communities introduced a new dimension, for it brought the country into a political system which has great influence – and perhaps more than influence – upon its constituent members. The European Economic Community Treaty in particular has superimposed what is very like another constitution upon Bunreacht na hÉireann.

Although the timing and direction of much constitutional change has been governed by shifts in Anglo-Irish relations, as Ireland moved towards autonomy and disassociation from the British Commonwealth that made necessary or opportune alterations in a definition of those relationships, the spirit and content of the Irish Constitutions also reflect a much more positive British influence. Britain's legacy to Ireland included a cultural inheritance and traditions, social and political institutions and patterns of services, and in total it was enormous. Moreover, political independence did not automatically end this transfer or bring economic or cultural independence. A separate and viable Irish economy emerged only gradually as banking, insurance, industry and trade became slowly centred upon Dublin: agriculture was even slower to change from being geared exclusively to British needs. The borders of the Irish state have always been highly permeable and people and ideas cross them with great ease. In 1981, 607,000 people born in the Republic of Ireland were resident in Great Britain, a figure equal to nearly one-fifth of the population of the Republic. British newspapers, particularly the Sunday papers, circulate in the Republic and, in 1985, about one-third of the adult population of the Republic regularly watched British television.

The British influence upon Ireland has certainly waned in recent years, particularly since accession to the European Communities. Nevertheless, it is still an important factor, not least in politics and in particular in inducing constitutional development. As most Irish people see it, there is still unfinished business while Northern Ireland remains part of the United Kingdom. Were the problem of Northern Ireland a matter only for the governments of the United Kingdom and the Republic, it might by now have been dealt with and appropriate constitutional changes made. However, the people – perhaps we should say the peoples – of the North itself are not at the disposal of the two governments if they could agree. If and when that problem is resolved, or perhaps as part of that resolution, there will have to be yet another in the series of constitutions that mark the changes in Ireland's relationship with the United Kingdom which is the subject of this chapter.

II

To understand Ireland, it is essential to view it, geographically, as an off-shore island of Great Britain, a small island with a much more populous neighbour; and, historically, reflecting the geographical situation, as part of the periphery of an English state which, because it was so successful in absorbing its neighbours, came to be called the United Kingdom. Irish history is the history of British domination that stopped short of absorption – unlike, for example, the case of Wales – and of subsequent national emancipation that was, however, not neatly and completely achieved with the emergence of an independent state in 1921.

Because of Ireland's proximity to Great Britain and its economic and strategic importance, it became and, until the twentieth century, remained essentially a province of the British homeland and not an overseas colony. The post-medieval British monarchs, typical of the absolute rulers of the time, sought to impose not only political control but social, economic and cultural conformity as well. To a degree they succeeded: Ireland became an integral part of the United Kingdom. The Irish economy was integrated with the British to serve mainly English ends. The Irish people absorbed much of the culture of the English, though most of them retained the Catholic faith which was to be a vital ingredient of nationalism in the nineteenth century.

Political and economic control and social and cultural absorption were aided by the practice of planting settlers and giving them land taken from the indigenous population. These settlers were English or Scottish in origin and Protestant in religion. A class of Protestant landowners and urban bourgeoisie developed who made up a distinct sub-culture, an elite who dominated Ireland until the late nineteenth century. In the context of the United Kingdom they were essentially provincials. The process was also aided by the ability of the United Kingdom to effect the transition to a rich, modern, industrialised country and to acquire an empire, successes which led the English to feel themselves and to be recognised by others as superior people whose habits, life style and culture generally should be emulated by lesser breeds.

This domination and cultural blanketing was particularly

obvious when it came to politics. The process of political modernisation led to the development of common political values throughout the British Isles, and Irish people shared these values and practised politics in a manner generally similar to the other peoples of these islands. The right to vote was extended in a succession of measures each following similar extensions on the mainland, and mass parties characteristic of modern democracy began to operate in Ireland as elsewhere. Irish politics was practised in the electoral, parliamentary and local government contexts of the British system and as part of it. Westminster with its unique traditions and customs was the parliamentary stage for Irish political actors and Dublin Castle, the centre of Irish public administration, housed a provincial administration. Much was devolved upon it, but it was obliged to look across the water for many policy decisions and for sanction to act in many matters great and small. There were ministers of cabinet rank directing Irish public business, but the control centre of the British administrative machine was in Whitehall and the Treasury mandarins at its heart were as concerned to save candle ends in Dublin as in London and Edinburgh.

Not only were political and administrative structures in Ireland largely similar to those in the rest of the United Kingdom, so too were public services. Ireland had special problems and sometimes received special treatment, but, in general, environmental, health and social services were extended in parallel with their development in Great Britain. In particular, universal primary education produced high levels of literacy.

By the end of the nineteenth century Ireland was in many respects a modern, developed western country whose people subscribed to a liberal-democratic ideology and expected to be provided with the same services and to enjoy the same rights as British people. Some of them insisted that their rights included the right to self-government and national independence. The mainstream of the Irish nationalist movement was liberal democratic in a markedly British way and conducted its campaign in the British political arena.

Despite the fact that, with the emergence of Sinn Féin, direct action was preferred to constitutional methods, most of the leaders envisaged that the independent Ireland for which they were struggling would be a republic with a parliamentary form of government. In keeping with the Sinn Féin policy of establishing the institutions of a separate state, this meant producing a constitution. Such a constitution would be, as one might say, by Irish nationalism out of British liberalism.

III

The members of the self-styled Dáil Éireann which convened in Dublin on 21 January 1919 claimed to be the legitimate representatives of the Irish people by virtue of having been directly elected, albeit to the British Parliament, at the general election of December 1918. The political tactics of the independence movement involved establishing at least the essential structures of a government and administration and inducing their fellow country men and women, with the help of the military wing if necessary, to recognise these and to repudiate British institutions. In order to emphasise the authenticity of their republicanism, they included among their very first parliamentary activities, the making and enacting of a constitution. That Constitution, together with a 'Declaration of Independence' and a 'Democratic programme' which, though not formally part of the Constitution, should be read with it, reaffirmed, and fleshed out the 'Proclamation of the Republic of Ireland' of Easter 1916.

In looking at the Constitution of Dáil Éireann 1919, it has to be remembered that it was a part of a political propaganda exercise by people who were in rebellion but were not social revolutionaries seeking to transform their community. In the circumstances in which they found themselves, they had no need for, and certainly no time to produce, a well-considered, polished legal document. They turned to what they knew and accepted. The political structures of their republic were to be those of British cabinet government. Five short articles covered the composition and competence of Dáil Éireann; the appointment and position of a prime minister and a government and their responsibility to the Dáil; the appointment of a chairman of the Dáil and the control and audit of public expenditure by the Dáil. 'A familiar and acceptable model – the Westminster model – was available and was simply taken over.'[1] Even the parliamentary procedures which they adopted, together with the language and terminology they used, were pure Westminster and so, too, were the Standing Orders of Dáil Éireann which revealed 'an almost total acceptance of the British pattern of legislative-executive relations'.[2]

Conversely, the other model of democratic government – republican government at that – which one might have expected to have been followed, the American, was not accepted. Despite De Valera's frequent references when in the United States to the affinity between the Irish and American Constitutions, he and his colleagues who led the movement pointedly rejected attempts to modify the system in that direction. A draft preamble to the Constitution beginning 'We, the people of Ireland ...' that obviously evoked the American prototype, was dropped. De Valera himself was not 'the President' (though usually addressed as such) but, according to the Constitution, 'Prime Minister (Priomh Aireach)'. An attempt to establish a President of the Republic who should be Prime Minister as well was not accepted. Likewise, attempts to confer more power upon the Dáil and make it more like Congress by having strong committees, and thus to modify the strong cabinet government of the British system, also failed. In this and other ways it was clear that 'Irish politics were to remain within a parliamentary mould; there was no support or even desire for a presidential system.'[3] What the founding fathers were doing on 21 January 1919 was patently symbolic and formal and much of the proceedings of that first parliament was political gesturing. Nevertheless, in fact, in Brian Farrell's words, they were establishing 'the constitutional cornerstone of the new Irish state; the origins of a cabinet system of government that has persisted to this day'.[4]

IV

The founding fathers of 1919 were concerned with forging political weapons for the struggle against the British government. The occasion of Ireland's next constitution, the Constitution of the Irish Free State (1922), was the success of that struggle, albeit a qualified success. It was a constitution for a *de facto* sovereign state, but it was not wholly 'Irish made' and the new state had willy-nilly to accept a special relationship with the United Kingdom.

The Provisional Government that took over in January 1922 was greatly constrained in formulating a constitution by the terms of the Treaty that had just been signed. It had, in addition, to bear in mind undertakings given to the leaders of the Protestant minority in which the British government also had an interest. The most important of the Treaty constraints concerned the constitutional status of the Irish Free State as a member of the British Commonwealth. In British eyes, this necessitated the inclusion of the symbols and institutions of government then considered appropriate for a Commonwealth country, in particular the recognition of the British monarch as head of state; a governor general as that monarch's representative; an oath of loyalty; and machinery of government modelled on the arrangements current in Commonwealth countries, particularly Canada.

Almost but not quite as important as far as the leaders of the time were concerned, was the position of the six northern counties, already identified as a separate political unit by the Government of Ireland Act, 1920. Under the Treaty, the parliamentary representatives of those counties were to have the right to decide whether to remain a part of the United Kingdom or to join the Irish Free State. Of course, they chose to remain. Other matters in the Treaty that had to be taken into account when framing the Constitution included a prohibition on imposing disabilities on account of religion, together with a guarantee for the free expression of religious beliefs and a prohibition on endowment; compensation for dismissed or retiring public servants; and the assumption of responsibility for a due proportion of the public debt. (There were also provisions to safeguard British security.) In order to satisfy the British government on these matters, it was necessary to consult it at the drafting stage and changes were made at its behest.

During the Treaty negotiations, pledges had also been given to safeguard the Unionist minority by giving them representation in the parliament of the new state. This obligation was honoured by adopting a proportional representation system of election (the single transferable vote system) and by arranging the membership of the Senate in such a way as to ensure over-representation of conservative elements in general and Unionists in particular. To copperfasten the provisions of the Treaty, a repugnancy clause (clause 2) in the Constitution of the Irish Free State Act (the act that enacted the Constitution and embodied it as a Schedule) provided that 'if any provision of the said Constitution or of any amendment thereof or of any law made thereunder is in any respect repugnant to any of the provisions of the scheduled Treaty, it shall ... be absolutely void and inoperative'.

The result of Irish leaders having to meet these requirements was that the Constitution contained a strange mixture of two different and antipathetic political traditions; the one republican, embodying the theory of popular sovereignty; the other the British political tradition of constitutional monarchy and Commonwealth status. To Hugh Kennedy, the first Attorney General of the Irish Free State, and those who thought like him, it was 'perfectly clear that fundamental sovereign authority proceeds from the people in the first instance to the elected representatives of Ireland in Dáil Éireann assembled',[5] and the Dáil itself enacted the Constitution 'in the exercise of undoubted right'.[6] To others reading the Treaty and the Constitution it was not so clear. The inclusion of the British monarch as part of the machinery of government and of the apparatus of Commonwealth status, though largely formal fictions, were in sharp contrast to the republican principles enunciated elsewhere. At the very least it involved a form of association distasteful to many and unacceptable to some.

These internal inconsistencies symbolised deep disagreements, both political and personal, that had great and lasting consequences. They precipitated a civil war that in turn generated the major political cleavage running through Irish politics to this day. This issue, a direct outcome of British policy, dominated – blighted might almost be a more appropriate word – the history of modern Ireland, the more so because the animosities it roused were exacerbated by the fact that this Constitution was the basic law for the state envisaged in the Treaty, namely a twenty-six county state that left Northern Ireland part of the United Kingdom. Thus was created the new state's second major problem. Accepted by De Valera and many others as insoluble in the short run – and certainly the British government had no alternative in the face of Unionist intransigence – partition generated typical irredentist attitudes in the twenty-six counties that further poisoned Anglo-Irish relations and limited the scope for cooperation. As time passed, it assumed greater importance. The issue was clearly posed in Ireland's next constitution, De Valera's Bunreacht na hÉireann (1937), and once the problems of constitutional status were solved with the formal declaration of a republic and exit from the Commonwealth after the Second World War, partition became the focus of Nationalist discontent.

The dangerous and occasionally lethal by-product of these disputed issues in Anglo-Irish relations has been a continuous succession of extreme nationalist subversive movements whose guerilla activities have kept security high on the agenda of all Irish governments and necessitated emergency legislation, special courts and wide state discretionary powers throughout the history of independent Ireland. It is important to recognise that the contemporary successors of this unbroken line of 'anti-system' groups – Sinn Féin, the Irish Republican Army and their even more extreme offshoots – do not only wage war in and over Northern Ireland. Like their predecessors right back to the 1920s, they do not recognise the authority of Irish governments any more than British, for they regard them as illegitimate.

The disparity in the constitutional provisions of the Irish Free State Constitution was to some degree repeated in the machinery of government clauses. Continuing the tradition established by Dáil Éireann in 1919, the system of government adopted was based in the main on the early-twentieth-century Westminster model. 'A bold attempt' was made 'to capture the essential elements of cabinet government and squeeze them into the phraseology of constitutional clauses'.[7] However, following the recommendations of a drafting committee bent on correcting what they saw as the imperfections of that model, there were included in the Irish Free State Constitution procedures and institutions intended to prevent strong governments from dominating parliament and the electorate. These included provisions for a referendum and the initiative, i.e. the right of citizens themselves to propose legislation, and for 'extern ministers', i.e. non-cabinet technocrat ministers directly responsible to the Dáil. Together with rules intended to boost the role of the Oireachtas and with the use of the single transferable vote system in multi-member constituencies, these made up a package intended to lessen the strength of cabinets *vis-à-vis* the Oireachtas, to promote a multi-party arrangement and generally to democratise the system.

It was a desire not shared by all of those in power and hardly practicable in the circumstances of the time with the new government struggling to establish the state in the face of unconstitutional opposition that extended to guerilla tactics. The split over the Treaty had polarised Irish politics and strong government in the Westminster style was the order of the day and, as it turned out, for generations. It was not just a matter of strong government however. To function properly a democracy requires an effective opposition. Here the role of the Labour Party in the first years and particularly of its leader, Tom Johnson, was crucial. A man in sympathy with, and thoroughly able to operate in, the Westminster style, he copperfastened parliamentary government until such time as

De Valera came to realise in the mid-1920s that the Irish were basically a constitutionalist people and led the main body of the anti-Treatyites into constitutional politics to assume the role of the official opposition party and alternative government.

Likewise, the rights of the individual included in the Constitution were mostly expressed in markedly British terms. Irish people, as we have observed, had adopted liberal values along with the British, and the enunciation of rights such as habeas corpus, free expression and the inviolability of the citizen's home all reflected this tradition in their content and tone. The concern for social welfare and the moderate socialist flavour that marked the constitutional documents of the Dáil era and echoed some of the post-war constitutions of western Europe were more muted in this Constitution for the radicals and socialists in the independence movement were not among those who had come to power in 1922.

More surprising perhaps, the strong connection between Irish nationalism and Catholicism was not reflected in the Constitution. In fact there is no mention of that or any church. The Irish government was bound by the Treaty not to endow any religion, not to discriminate on account of religious belief and to protect the property of all churches but, as John Whyte observed, 'it does not follow that this obligation was accepted reluctantly'.[8] On the contrary, the authors went further and retained what Whyte has identified as the 'Anglo-American' tradition of aloofness in Church–state relations as opposed to the more 'European' pattern of state support. They produced 'a typical liberal-democratic document which would have suited a country of any religious complexion'.[9]

Just as the text of the Irish Free State Constitution is hardly intelligible except in the context of Anglo-Irish relations, so too its development was almost wholly a matter, on the one hand, of continuing the process of pulling away from the British connection and, on the other, of confirming the suitability of the Westminster model to the needs of the Irish whose political socialisation had been so strongly influenced by British attitudes and practices. The Constitution was much amended. The Cumann na nGaedheal governments of the 1920s did not hesitate to alter the machinery of government as necessity dictated and convenience or experience suggested. The 'un-British' constitutional devices were sloughed off or were never used and, by the late 1920s, the institutions and practices of Irish government were firmly established along the Westminster lines of strong cabinet government and puny parliaments: to a great extent that is still the position today.

In respect of the constitutional status of the country, however, the Cumann na nGaedheal leaders felt bound by the Treaty and the Constitution as agreed with the British and enacted. Instead of seeking changes unilaterally, they tried 'to refashion the Commonwealth in closer accord with Irish interests and outlook'.[10] They made some impact too; one of the few examples of reverse influence in the Anglo-Irish experience. By contrast, Fianna Fáil, from 1927 the major opposition party in the Dáil, were dedicated to loosening and if possible severing Irish ties with the Commonwealth. Once De Valera took office, a radical revision of the Constitution was inevitable. It would involve, firstly, the removal from the Irish Free State Constitution by amendment of the symbols and procedures of Commonwealth status and, then, the making of a new constitution that would be 'unquestionably indigenous in character'.[11] It would mark another step in the process of disentangling Ireland from the British system. Otherwise, apart from a more explicit recognition of the Catholic nature of the country, little would be changed, for the values and practices of liberal democracy in the British style were unquestionably 'indigenous' to the Irish people, as experience in the first decade of independence had demonstrated.

v

Just as the Irish Free State Constitution marked a stage in the struggle of the Irish to detach themselves from the United Kingdom and was a compromise, so too did Bunreacht na hÉireann (The Constitution of Ireland) 1937. However, whereas the former was a product of a war and a negotiated treaty and, on the Irish side, embodied the compromises that *one* part of the independence movement could live with, the latter reflected more the aspirations of the *other* part of that movement and the compromises that they would tolerate. More accurately they were those of the leader of that section, De Valera, for Bunreacht na hÉireann was to a great extent *his* Constitution. In it, he sought to justify his consistent stand from the winter of 1921–22 and to realise as far as possible *his* version of Anglo-Irish relations. He had already embarked on his mission by effecting a number of amendments of the Irish Free State Constitution that removed offending sections and, by taking the opportunity of the crisis that led to the abdication of King Edward VIII in 1936, to remove references to the monarch from the Constitution.

Although this was very much De Valera's Constitution, it does not follow that the provisions embodied in it were his ideal vision of the Irish state. This would have been a state that was unequivocally republican, thirty-two county, Catholic and Gaelic. However, fifteen years on from the Treaty he recognised the constraints within which he had to operate in respect of links with the United Kingdom, if only for security and economic reasons. He was also alive to the problem he faced – even if he did not fully understand it – in seeking to include Northern Unionists in an all-Ireland state, particularly if that state was to have some of the characteristics he so much desired. He was not producing the basic law for a united country, but for the peoples of two political units, one still a province of a powerful neighbour state. He had always accepted that there had to be a special relationship between the two countries and that in the short run at least he could at best complete but another stage, albeit a vital one in his eyes, in what would be a long haul towards a satisfactory definition of that relationship.

If the influence of British policy and the attitudes of those ultra-British, the Northern Ireland Unionists, fixed the parameters on the one side, scarcely less important were the demands of the most extreme nationalists in his own party and the need to try to placate or upstage the extremists in Sinn Féin, the IRA and other ultra-nationalist groups. Their aims – a thirty-two county republic at once – were simplistic and unattainable but were capable of arousing great public emotion, and De Valera was very conscious of this. This was the parameter within which he was constrained on the other side. The consequence was that Bunreacht na hÉireann like its predecessor embodied compromises and had its equivocations.

Bunreacht na hÉireann was essentially a constitution for a republic. The very first words indicated that: 'We, the people of Éire, ... do hereby adopt, enact and give to ourselves this Constitution'. With this declaration and with the provision for an elected president in place of the monarch, De Valera was rejecting Commonwealth status as it was understood at the time and abrogating the Treaty; and this was his intention. However, nowhere was there a statement declaring explicitly that the state was a republic: this too was deliberate. Instead, Article 4 stated that 'the name of the state is Éire or in the English language Ireland': not, be it noted, Poblacht na hÉireann, (the Republic of Ireland), the designation used in the Proclamation of the Republic at Easter, 1916. Likewise, the article that characterises the state, Article 5, declares only that 'Ireland is a sovereign, independent, democratic state'.

This equivocation resulted in a decade of doubt and debate about the status of the state. De Valera, however, was adamant that what was being done suited exactly the circumstances and opportunities of the time. 'If the Northern problem were not there', he told Dáil Éireann, 'in all probability there would be a flat downright proclamation of a republic ....'[12] However, it was there, as intransigent and insoluble as ever. To have gone further would, he maintained, have made a satisfactory resolution all the more difficult. This was the by now familiar dilemma of Nationalist leaders. From December 1921 onwards, De Valera had recognised the need for the Irish state to remain associated with the United Kingdom and this policy of 'external association' as opposed to Commonwealth membership, together with recognition of the British monarch for the limited purposes of that association (defence, peace and war, treaty making etc.), became and remained his strategy for achieving the Nationalists' disparate aims. The arrangement devised in 1936 in the Executive Authority (External Relations) Act was continued, though it was couched in obscure language in Article 29:

For the purpose of the exercise of any executive function of the State in or in connection with its external relations, the Government may ... avail of or adopt any organ, instrument, or method of procedure used or adopted for the like purpose by the members of any group or league of nations with which the State is or becomes associated for the purpose of international cooperation in matters of common concern.

From the end of December 1937, the Irish state, which quickly became known as Éire, was in Irish law at least no longer a member of the Commonwealth; the monarch was no longer head of state; and the British crown was used only for accrediting diplomatic representatives.

De Valera's strategy in respect of Northern Ireland, in his own words 'a policy of patience and opportunism',[13] is precisely reflected in the wording of Articles 2 and 3. Article 2 is declaratory and makes a juridical claim: 'the national territory consists of the whole island of Ireland, its islands and the territorial seas'. Article 3 recognises the reality of the situation and provides for it: 'Pending the reintegration of the national territory ..., the laws [of the state] shall have the like area and extent of application as the laws of Saorstát Éireann [the Irish Free State]'. This was to pose the issue in the most formal way: the problem was still on the back burner, but the heat was perhaps being turned up a little. If and when the major problem, the constitutional status of the state, was satisfactorily resolved, it would inevitably get more attention. However, it would not then necessarily be the more soluble: quite the contrary, for any solution of the constitutional issue could not but alienate Northern Unionists even further. The treatment of these issues in Bunreacht na hÉireann itself already contributed to that result.

The truth was that De Valera's policy was doomed to failure. His ultimate objectives were mutually incompatible, though neither he nor most of his contemporaries recognised this. Consequently, even in matters where he had more elbow room and had not to walk a tightrope between extremes of nationalism, Irish and Ulster, he took up stands that would strengthen the resolve of Unionists to have nothing to do with 'Southern Ireland' and copperfasten partition. Prominent among these were religion and the Irish language.

In order to allay Protestant fears, the Irish Free State Constitution (1922) contained declarations prohibiting the state from endorsing any religion, from discrimination on account of religious belief and from acquiring church property by compulsion except for certain public works and then only with compensation. The rights it guaranteed were the classic liberal rights that were an established feature of the British tradition which, as we have seen, Ireland shared. However, both the governments of that era (1922–37), Cumann na nGaedheal and Fianna Fáil, were inclined to bring state law into line with contemporary Catholic teaching. De Valera himself was a devout Catholic who saw Ireland as essentially a Catholic nation: Bunreacht na hÉireann would make it unequivocally a Catholic state.

The Catholic influence is to be seen particularly in some of the rights articles, notably in Article 41 (on the family), Article 42 (on education), Article 43 (on private property) and Article 44 (on religion). Elsewhere also it can be seen in Article 45 (Directive Principles of Social Policy) and in the provisions for vocational representation which reflected a papal enthusiasm of the time. These provisions based on Catholic teaching are combined with the liberal-democratic provisions retained from the Irish Free State Constitution. Thus Bunreacht na hÉireann conflates principles from the two traditions which have most influenced Irish life. Often regarded as antipathetic, their combination in this Constitution suited Irish people and served them well, at least until recently.

With Article 44, however, De Valera was back with his

perennial dilemma – how to realise his Catholic nationalist objectives and yet avoid alienating Northern Protestant Unionists. How was he to stifle their conviction and allay their fear that 'home rule is Rome rule' while at the same time complying with contemporary Catholic church teaching that it was the duty of the state to make a public profession of the Catholic religion? His solution – and it was of his own devising in face of considerable pressure by clerics – was to have the state recognise 'the special position of the Holy Catholic Apostolic and Roman Church as the guardian of the Faith professed by the great majority of the citizens' while according recognition also to the other churches that existed in the state at the time.

This formula was less than ideal as far as Catholic teaching was concerned. Nevertheless, although it was acceptable to Southern Protestants, it went much too far for Northern Protestants. As Conor Cruise O'Brien observed, if De Valera was, as he said he was, concerned to woo the north, Articles 2, 3 and 44 were 'an odd bouquet to choose.... It would be hard to think of a combination of propositions more likely to sustain and stiffen the siege mentality of protestant Ulster'.[14] For thirty years or more, few in the Republic were able and willing to recognise this.

Likewise the Irish language, a subject about which he sometimes said he felt more strongly than about a united Ireland. Here again he did not go as far as might have been expected. There is no attempt in Bunreacht na hÉireann to force the use of the language as has occurred in some nationally self-conscious states. The Irish language as 'the national language' is recognised as the first official language with English as 'a second official language' and has priority in certain situations. Apparently, he 'had no fear that his dream of restoring Irish would run counter in any way to his other dream – the reuniting of the country'.[15] In truth, they were both pipe-dreams. The one mattered very little to the Northern Unionists only because they did not take Irish seriously; the other mattered very much. It would not be long before that dream became for them a nightmare.

For the moment, however, the constitutional issue – what De Valera in 1921 had called 'the big question' – continued to have precedence. Although he took the increased opportunities that occurred to raise the partition issue in the troubled times that followed, it was never allowed to stand in the way of achieving other objectives or to generate crises in Anglo-Irish relations.

The treatment of constitutional issues in Bunreacht na hÉireann was designed, according to De Valera, to put 'the question of our international relations in their proper place – and that is outside the Constitution'.[16] In his view, his formulations permitted easy passage towards the desired goal, since not one word of the Constitution would need to be altered to break the link with the United Kingdom and to declare the state formally a republic if and when it became opportune to do so. He was quite right, for the next stage in the evolution of the Irish state, although undoubtedly a major constitutional change, necessitated no amendment of Bunreacht na hÉireann itself. When in 1948 John A. Costello's Inter-Party (i.e. coalition) Government decided to break the link, it was sufficient to repeal the Executive Authority (External Relations) Act, to assign all executive powers in connection with foreign affairs to the President acting on the advice of the government and to declare that 'the description of the state shall be the Republic of Ireland', all of which were done by ordinary legislation in the Republic of Ireland Act, 1948. With this act and with the formal acknowledgement by the governments of the Commonwealth, including the United Kingdom government, that Éire, as they called it, was no longer a member of the Commonwealth, Ireland's status as a republic was finally formalised and universally acknowledged. Thus ended what irreverent opponents of De Valera called the policy of 'exclude me in and include me out'.

The enactment of the Republic of Ireland Act, 1948, and the symbolic declaration of a republic on Easter day 1949, though undoubtedly salutary were full of irony. Firstly, it was his political opponents and not De Valera himself who made the change. Indeed, although he did not – could not – oppose it publicly, he had doubts about its wisdom, for he feared that it might harm the cause of unity by destroying a bridge to the North.[17]

Secondly, it marked the end of the policy of 'external association', the attempt to explore the possibilities of establishing an intimate relationship between a republic and the British Commonwealth whose unifying symbol had always been the British monarch. Yet at the very time when this possibility was extinguished for Ireland, it was being realised successfully by other states then emerging to independence from the British empire.

Thirdly, although so far as the world of states was concerned, the United Kingdom was now a 'foreign' state in Ireland and vice-versa, in practice this could hardly be the case. The Ireland Act, 1949 (an Act of the British Parliament) declared the Republic of Ireland not to be a foreign country and Irish citizens were not to be classed as aliens but to continue to have the exemptions contained in the British Nationality Act. Since then they have in fact enjoyed privileges beyond those of Commonwealth citizens. In this and in many other ways a uniquely close association was and continues to be recognised to the material advantage of the peoples of both countries.

Finally, it is bitterly ironic to recall that events in Northern Ireland since 1948 have made nonsense of the expressed hopes of the leaders of the time that the declaration of a republic would 'take the gun out of Irish politics'. On the contrary, the settlement of 'the big question' led to the advancement of the Northern problem from the back burner to the forefront of Anglo-Irish relations. The stirring of that pot has had tragic consequences. Never have there been more guns in Irish politics.

That the solution of one of Ireland's national problems would exacerbate the other was, however, inevitable. For, whether it was tackled from the traditional assumptions of Irish Nationalists – one nation; a British injustice; soluble by British government action – or in the light of a more realistic appreciation of the existence and legitimacy of two traditions, both of which must be accommodated, that generally developed from the 1960s, an agreed solution to the Northern problem was probably unattainable. The pages of recent Irish and British constitutional history are littered with statements of irreconcilable positions and failed constitutional schemes. Meanwhile, the activities of those who choose to pursue nationalist objectives by direct action have been equally futile though infinitely more corrosive and counter-productive.

What has become increasingly clear is that any solution would require the amendment or replacement of Bunreacht na hÉireann as one of its components. The authors of the *Report of the Committee on the Constitution* (1967) were the first to dare to tackle the issue of amending Articles 2 and 3, but that report had hastily to be buried because many, particularly in Fianna Fáil, were not prepared, as they saw it, to betray De Valera and subvert his hallowed Constitution. The issue of when and in what circumstances to amend or replace Bunreacht na hÉireann to make the republican house ready for the Northern bride has become and remains a live issue in Irish politics not only because of Articles 2 and 3 but also because of the need to accommodate changing and divergent attitudes to divorce and other moral issues.

Thus Ireland's next constitution, like all its predecessors, might be occasioned by a change – actual, intended or putative – in the Northern Ireland situation, in other words in Anglo-Irish relations. The Hillsborough Agreement (1985), like the Republic of Ireland Act in 1948, made what were in effect constitutional changes, albeit very modest changes only intended as a first step, without an amendment of Bunreacht na hÉireann. Any 'solution' of the northern problem would require constitutional changes not only in the relations of the Republic with Northern Ireland but also of the Republic with the United Kingdom as a whole on a scale that would necessitate recasting Bunreacht na hÉireann.

However, the impact of the Hillsborough agreement upon Northern Unionist opinion underlines once again that, as in the past when British ministers and governments seemed in principle willing to 'trade off' Northern Ireland for some other policy objective, their room for manoeuvre is limited by ultra-Unionist determination never to allow Northern Ireland to be grafted on to an Irish Republic. The Northern Ireland problem is not a problem that can be solved by the two governments however sovereign they consider themselves to be. Perhaps the engine that has powered constitutional change in the Irish state for seventy years has come to a halt.

VI

There are other engines and they are getting up steam. On the one hand, a growing public desire for social reform and, on the other, the obligations of membership of the European Communities both raise constitutional issues. They reflect the fact that people's horizons have widened. In the last ten to twenty years, Irish people have come increasingly to see this country in a context wider than that of an off-shore island of Great Britain.

The great changes in Irish society induced by a surge of industrialisation and urbanisation and by the resultant rapid rise in living standards from the early 1960s led to the spread of life styles resembling those of rich industrial countries. The inexorable change in people's values that were a consequence of this, combined with the changes in the stance of the Roman Catholic Church initiated by the second Vatican Council and the increase in television viewing, led to growing debate on matters that hitherto had been seen as settled, among them marriage and divorce, contraception, abortion and relations with other religions. People began to adopt a more independent attitude to their clergy and to question rules and relationships that they thought were appropriate only to a rural peasant society. From the early 1960s pluralistic and secular attitudes began to spread. As they did so, issues with constitutional implications inevitably arose.

In 1972, the section of Article 44 of Bunreacht na hÉireann that accorded recognition of 'the special position' of the Roman Catholic Church was removed by amendment after

Cardinal Conway had given the nod on behalf of the Church. Issues like contraception, divorce, abortion and inter-denominational education have proved more contentious. Divorce in particular has been the subject of continuous debate as efforts have been made to get the ban on the Oireachtas passing any law 'providing for the grant of a dissolution of marriage' removed from Article 41 of the Constitution. More generally, a growing awareness of the attitudes and practices of western Europe in respect of human rights, together with decisions of European courts (under the European Convention of Human rights and the Treaty of Rome) are having a growing impact on Irish public opinion. As rights are recognised or the obligation to respect them forced on Irish society by international law or treaty obligations, the need to revise the Constitution to incorporate them will become more pressing.

Some of these rights issues arise in the context of the European Economic Community, but Ireland's accession in 1972 raised altogether wider constitutional issues that have never been wholly satisfactorily resolved. The European Economic Community is 'a new type of international organisation with much greater powers over member countries than those traditionally given to international institutions'.[18] Ireland's move to join in the early 1970s raised questions about amending Bunreacht na hÉireann to make accession legally possible and to bring it into harmony with the body of Community law that would have to be received. As it stood, the Constitution required that the state should determine for itself to what extent and how it will receive international law: the obligations of Community membership required otherwise. Community 'regulations' and 'decisions' apply directly in member states and are binding on all to whom they apply including the state itself. Community 'directives' oblige states 'to bring about a specified result [although] the choice of form and methods of carrying out objectives is left to the national authorities'.[19] Furthermore, the Treaty of Rome requires domestic courts to uphold rights and obligations under the Treaties and the European Court stands alongside, and in some circumstances above, domestic courts.

The way to Ireland's accession was cleared by the simplest of all possible means – by tacking an enabling clause on to Article 29.4 of the Constitution. The Third Amendment to the Constitution Act, 1972 provided that

> the State may become a member of [the Communities] ... no provision of this Constitution invalidates laws enacted, acts done or measures adopted by the Communities, or institutions thereof, from having the force of law in the State.

The Treaties, and in particular the Treaty of Rome, became in effect Ireland's second Constitution. It was a major constitutional change to which, for the first time in Irish experience, the United Kingdom had contributed little. Nevertheless, British influence was not absent. Ireland joined the Communities when it did because the United Kingdom was also joining. Given the close economic links there was no desirable alternative. In the future perhaps that influence would be less pervasive precisely because of the European connection and, indeed, this argument was used to sell the proposal in Ireland.

The simple addition to Article 29 was undoubtedly the easiest way of coping with the problems of possible conflict of laws. The result, though, is that the actual position in respect of a number of matters dealt with in the Constitution is not what the Constitution appears to say it is. It might be argued that if there exists a source of law, including fundamental law, other than the domestic sources, Bunreacht na hÉireann itself ought periodically to be amended to effect the necessary harmonisation and to incorporate explicitly the rights and obligations created by Community organs.

As yet, Irish governments have not paid much attention to these matters. Although Irish people are not now so obsessed with the British connection and other influences are increasingly being felt as horizons widen, many Irish political leaders still tend to see constitutional development in the context of the Northern Ireland problem. Because there is no acceptable solution to that problem its influence is negative and inhibitory.

REFERENCES

1. Brian Farrell, *The Founding of Dáil Éireann: Parliament and Nation Building* (Dublin, 1971), p. xviii.
2. Farrell, *The Founding*, p. 68.
3. Farrell, *The Founding*, p. 74.
4. Farrell, *The Founding*, p. 51.
5. Quoted Farrell, *The Founding*, p. 67.
6. Preamble to the Constitution of the Irish Free State (Saorstát Éireann) Act, No 1 of 1922.
7. F. A. Ogg, *English Government and Politics* (New York, 1936), 2nd edn, p. 731.
8. J. Whyte, *Church and State in Modern Ireland, 1923–79*, (Dublin, 1980), 2nd edn, p. 14.
9. Whyte, *Church and State*, p. 51.
10. N. Mansergh, *Survey of British Commonwealth Affairs: Problems of External Policy, 1931–1939* (London, 1952), p. 184. D. W. Harkness (*The Restless Dominion*, London and Dublin, 1969) stresses the leading part played by Irish leaders in preparing the way for the important redefinition of Commonwealth status embodied in the Statute of Westminster, 1931.
11. Mansergh, *Survey*, p. 307.
12. *Dáil Debates*, Vol. 68, Col. 430 (14 June 1937).
13. See John Bowman, *De Valera and the Ulster Question, 1917–1973* (Oxford, 1982), pp 282–3.
14. C. Cruise O'Brien, *States of Ireland* (St Albans, 1974), p. 116
15. The Earl of Longford and T. P. O'Neill, *Eamon De Valera* (Dublin and London, 1970), pp. 459–60.
16. *Dáil Debates*, Vol. 67–68, Col. 60 (11 May 1937).
17. See John Bowman, *op. cit.*, p. 273.
18. J. Temple Lang, *The Common Market and Common Law* (Chicago and London, 1966), p. xi.
19. Temple Lang, *The Common Market*, p. 10.

3 · Britain's legacy: government and administration

RONAN FANNING

The size of the British legacy of government and administration to independent Ireland must be set in the context of her political disinheritance. The Irish revolutionaries who fought against British forces during the war of independence were not, of course, disinherited by the British. They chose to disinherit themselves.

Their disinheritance was in two parts. First, Sinn Féin's rejection of the seventy-three seats they won in the Westminster parliamentary election of November 1918. The point has been most resonantly made by Winston Churchill:

> Not for a moment did they weigh or value the immense influence and leverage they could exert, for ill or for good upon the decisive affairs of the British Empire. 'Sinn Féin', 'Ourselves alone', that was the cry, and by an act of self-abnegation, remarkable even when born of hatred, they cut themselves off forever from an inheritance in the House of Commons which, though invidious, was in a worldly sense inestimable.[1]

The second part of that disinheritance was the rejection of the Home Rule legacy embodied in the Government of Ireland Act of 1920. This fourth and final Home Rule Bill brought forward by a British government failed not because of the disagreement it provoked among British political parties – which was why the earlier bills of 1886, 1893 and 1912 had never been implemented – but because Home Rule no longer satisfied those Irish nationalist aspirations which had first called it into existence fully forty years before.

But, although Sinn Féin within (and the IRA without) the Dáil of 1919–21 rejected the right of the British to rule Ireland, they did not reject the system of government and administration whereby that rule was exercised. While 'they repudiated the claim of Westminster to represent Ireland and the right of Whitehall to govern Ireland ... they were not attempting any more radical restructuring of Irish institutions and society'.[2]

The 'orders of the day' for the preparatory meeting for the convocation of Dáil Éireann held at the Mansion House in Dublin on 7 January 1919 reveal in embryo that concern with proper, and essentially British, parliamentary procedure which so quickly characterised the Dáil's proceedings.[3] The Standing Orders of the first Dáil are likewise imbued with a spirit of reverence for British practice and display 'an almost total acceptance of the British pattern of legislative-executive relations'.[4] So, too, does the first Constitution of Dáil Éireann, Article 2 of which gives the 'President of the Ministry' the right to nominate and to dismiss his fellow-ministers whose titles ('Secretary of Finance', 'Secretary of Home Affairs' etc.) similarly show their British origins. The same Article – 2 (c) – enunciates the British doctrine that 'every member of the Ministry shall be a member of Dáil Éireann, and shall at all times be responsible to the Dáil'.[5] The revised version, as amended on 25 August 1921, carries devotion to British nomenclature still further. The terms 'Ministry' and 'Secretary' are abandoned in favour of 'Cabinet' and 'Secretary of State' respectively and it is also laid down that 'the President shall also be Prime Minister'.[6]

The internal logic of the Dáil's rejection of the British right to rule Ireland demanded that its members behave almost as if there was no British presence in Ireland. And this was what they did. Although the Dáil cabinet met almost weekly between May 1919 and December 1920 their minutes only rarely hint that there was an ever-escalating guerilla war in progress or that the British denied the Dáil's authority.[7]

Nor should we forget how much the IRA's organisation and training owed to British example and how much of their expertise was gleaned from men who had received their military training in the British forces during the First World War. 'For me it began in far-off Mesopotamia ...

when I was serving with the Mesopotamian Expeditionary Force' is how Tom Barry begins his memoir of the Anglo-Irish war[8] and other examples abound.

The insistence, in August 1919, that all members of the IRA swear allegiance to the Dáil and the Dáil's subsequent assumption of responsibility, in March 1921, for all the actions of the IRA are further illustrations of the commitment to the British doctrine of parliamentary sovereignty. 'The army and the government of a country could not be under separate authority', insisted Arthur Griffith as acting-President; 'if they were a regularly constituted government there could be no question about the taking of an oath of allegiance'.[9]

The significance of these self-imposed limitations adopted by Irish revolutionaries has been well summarised by Brian Farrell:

the political, constitutional and legal underpinnings were nurtured as carefully, perhaps more carefully, than the demands and occasional local claims of fighting men in the field. Sinn Féin, after 1916, followed the political policy laid out before then by Griffith: to gain a popular electoral mandate and on this build a rival structure of government. Whereas the more usual strategy of national independence movements in the twentieth century involved a direct assault on and confrontation with existing structures of law and order, Sinn Féin tended rather to substitute a new set of structures. But these new structures and institutions followed the same pattern, and were based on the same values as the old. The same sources of legitimacy were claimed, the same representative functions exercised, the same model of cabinet government with its conventions of parliamentary responsibility and answerability adopted.[10]

One attempt to depart from British practice was the introduction of a resolution in September 1920 to bring the Dáil's constitution 'into harmony with the American idea of committees elected by the whole House and clothed with similar powers'. But it was opposed by Arthur Griffith and Eoin MacNeill (who described it as 'a very revolutionary proposal'!) and it failed ignominiously.[11] Enough has been said to show that the Irish revolutionaries' fidelity to British models was well established before the conclusion of the Anglo-Irish treaty of 6 December 1921 which paved the way for the foundation of an independent Irish state. But one further aspect of Dáil government in the pre-treaty period merits particular attention: the personal and departmental primacy established by the Dáil's Minister of Finance, Michael Collins.

Finance was from the beginning listed as the first of the ministries set out in Dáil Éireann's constitution. Its key role in raising the revenue to prosecute the guerilla war and to pay for the Dáil administration – the National Loan which Collins launched brought in over £370,000 between June 1919 and September 1920[12] – was one reason for its continued primacy. Much more important, however, was Collins's personal ascendancy over his ministerial colleagues and the way he used that ascendancy to implement certain conceptions of government which both anticipated and complemented the longstanding British principle of Treasury control. One instance of Collins's attention to administrative propriety at the height of the Anglo-Irish war was his appointment of an Accountant General, George McGrath, and his establishment within the Dáil Department of Finance of an Audit and Accounts Department – McGrath subsequently became the first Comptroller and Auditor-General of the Irish Free State.[13] In February 1920 Collins also established the principle that Finance matters should 'in future . . . be the first business taken up at Ministry meetings'.[14]

But the most important Dáil cabinet decision mirroring British practice and anticipating the cabinet procedure of the Irish Free State was taken on 30 September 1921 in the more relaxed atmosphere which prevailed after the July truce had brought an end to the Anglo-Irish war. It was then agreed that 'in future notice of any financial proposal to be brought up at Cabinet . . . be sent to (the) Finance Minister and, in general, any Minister intending to raise matters, that are strictly the business of a department other than his own should notify the minister of that department'.[15]

Collins similarly insisted on the British principle of ministerial accountability for the actions of civil servants and instructed that 'all communications' to his Department 'should be addressed simply "Aireacht Airgid" and not to any individual'.[16] He also fiercely opposed 'the practice of having members of the Dáil also officials of Departments' on the grounds that it would expose the Dáil cabinet 'to charges of jobbery, and with good reason' and he told De Valera that he thought the practice 'indefensible'.[17]

Collins's success in establishing financial control over other Dáil departments coupled with his determination to rid the Dáil administration of any taint of patronage or jobbery made for a climate favourable to the introduction of the British principle of Treasury control. And we should note that the principle had been powerfully reinforced in 1919 when it was announced that the Permanent Secretary of the Treasury would henceforth act as the Permanent Head of the Civil Service. A Treasury circular of 1920 further underlined their 'special relationship with the Premier and consolidat[ed] the Treasury's authority over the civil service'.[18]

The Great War had cruelly exposed the deficiencies in a creaking and antiquated British government machine. The result was that the eighteen months immediately preceding the Treaty witnessed the Treasury

> engaged in reorganising the whole of the civil service in England and Scotland as well as in Ireland ... Every single question of reorganisation which arose in Ireland was considered and decided by the Treasury on exactly the same principles as are being applied simultaneously in London ...
>
> The Treasury regarded it as part of their duty to hand over the Irish Civil Service in a good working order, with their staffs thoroughly overhauled and placed on a proper footing as regards pay, grading, number and conditions of tenure and service.[19]

In other words the civil service machine which the British government handed over had just been modernised and overhauled. The civil servants who ran that machine were fully aware of those reforms and their awareness gave the British administrative legacy even greater durability in the decades ahead.

But the crucial factor ensuring that the Provisional Government, entrusted with the task of preparing for the establishment of the Irish Free State between January and December 1922, would wholeheartedly accept that legacy was the prevailing political climate when they came into their inheritance.

That climate was characterised by schism and suspicion. The Treaty split and the consequent fears of civil war (especially after the anti-Treaty elements in the IRA occupied the Four Courts and other buildings in Dublin from mid-April 1922) immediately threatened the authority of the Provisional Government. The principal preoccupation of Michael Collins, now chairman of the Provisional Government as well as Minister of Finance, was to prove that he and his colleagues could govern. The main objective of their political opponents was to stop them governing.

On 16 January 1922 the process of administrative transition had begun when the British handed over Dublin Castle. Three days later the Provisional Government issued a statement announcing that they were completing the takeover of all departments and offices hitherto administered by the British. The statement stressed that minimum inconvenience would be caused to the public and that 'all existing Departments will continue to perform their normal functions except in so far as changes may be ordered from time to time in the public interest'.[20] The exception proved the rule. Change was to be subordinated to continuity in the government and administration of independent Ireland. Michael Collins and his colleagues wanted only to implement an administrative takeover, not to launch an administrative revolution.

Once the civil war began, on 28 June 1922, this concern for continuity was mightily reinforced. The siege mentality of ministers is apparent in Kevin O'Higgins's celebrated description of the Provisional Government as 'simply eight young men in the City Hall standing amidst the ruins of one administration, with the foundations of another not yet laid, and with wild men screaming through the keyhole'.[21] The 'wild men' were now the enemy. The British, in stark contrast, appeared as allies. It was no time for tinkering with the machinery of government, still less for discarding it, merely because it had previously been used by the British.

Nor did the civil war dispose the new owners of such machinery to learn to run it themselves. Such matters were best left to the experienced mechanics who came with the machinery. One of the most senior of those mechanics – Jimmy McElligott who, as Secretary of the Department of Finance, effectively presided over the Irish civil service from 1927 until 1953 – offered the opinion in later life that the one beneficial effect of the civil war was the opportunity it gave senior civil servants to install the administrative machinery of independent Ireland without the meddlesome interference of politicians.[22]

There were many such mechanics – the 20,415 civil servants who transferred from the service of the United Kingdom to the service of the Provisional Government on 1 April 1922 and who comprised more than 98 per cent of what became the civil service of the Irish Free State. Another eighty-eight appointees had also worked for the British civil service in Ireland but had resigned or been dismissed on political grounds during the revolutionary years. The balance was made up of a mere 131 officials who had worked for Dáil Éireann before the Treaty.

One reason which made for a good working relationship between civil servants and their new political masters was that the hard-core Unionist element had been effectively ousted from Dublin Castle *before* 1922. This process had begun in the spring of 1920 after an inspection by Sir Warren Fisher, the Permanent Secretary to the Treasury and head of the United Kingdom civil service. The Castle administration, Fisher told British cabinet ministers, was 'almost woodenly stupid and quite devoid of imagination. It listens solely to the ascendancy party'.[23] The outcome was the forced retirement of Sir John Taylor (the Assistant Under-Secretary and arch-Unionist) and the introduction of a team of some dozen high-flying British civil servants led by Sir John Anderson. Anderson was arguably the ablest civil servant the

British system produced in the twentieth century – he also made the transition to successful politician, becoming Governor of Bengal, Home Secretary, Chancellor of the Exchequer and the man entrusted with the task of negotiating with the Americans about atomic secrets during the Second World War.[24] He presided over the weeding out of Unionist and other deadwood in the Castle's higher reaches and the preparations for a smooth transfer of power with ruthless efficiency.

The transfer of services to Northern Ireland under the terms of the Government of Ireland Act of 1920 offered another opportunity to get rid of Dublin officials antipathetic to the political aspirations of their new masters. Some 300 volunteers transferred to Belfast between January and May 1922.[25] Another factor contributing to the same end was the provision in the 1920 Act,[26] reiterated in Article 10 of the Treaty that 'fair compensation' be paid to officials who retired 'in consequence of the change of government'. A total of 1,281 civil servants retired in consequence of the change of government during the 1920s: 728 in 1922–23, 209 in 1924, 43 in 1925 and a mere 15 between 1926 and 1929.[27]

The relations of two particular officials (Jimmy McElligott and Joe Brennan, McElligott's predecessor as Secretary of the Department of Finance from 1923 to 1927) with revolutionary nationalists in the pre-treaty period merit special attention. McElligott's Republican credentials were impeccable. An honours graduate in classics of University College, Dublin, he had been appointed as a First Division Clerk in the Local Government Board in 1913. His earliest years in the civil service were unremarkable but on Easter Monday, 1916, he sought and obtained admission to the GPO while returning from Fairyhouse races. He ended up in Stafford Jail in the cell beside Michael Collins and was summarily dismissed from the civil service on the recommendation of a committee set up to investigate the cases of civil servants suspected of involvement in the Easter Rising. He worked as a financial journalist in London from 1919 until 1922 (when he was again arrested 'for reconnoitring Chequers when

Lloyd George was in residence'). Then, in 1923, he was reinstated with the rank of assistant secretary in the Department of Finance.[28]

At first sight Brennan's early career seemed much more orthodox. Another First Division Clerk educated at Clongowes, University College, Dublin and Cambridge, he had been quickly plucked out for preferment and transferred to the Finance Division of Dublin Castle in 1912. Although his politics were of the 'Redmondite home ruler' variety, he found himself sucked into Michael Collins's circle when Patrick McGilligan (a former schoolmate of Brennan's at Clongowes) was instrumental in persuading him secretly to produce a series of financial memoranda for Collins's use in the Treaty negotiations – this at a time when Brennan was still working in Dublin Castle.[29] But then Brennan's disenchantment at the wanton and brutal behaviour of the Crown forces in 1920–21, particularly in his home town of Bandon, well reflected the increasing polarisation of Irish political opinion in these years.[30]

Brennan's and McElligott's connections with the revolutionary world should warn us against making too rigid a distinction between the mentalities of the neo-revolutionaries of the Provisional Government and the civil servants who had formerly worked for the British. It explains, too, why Michael Collins was so uninhibited about recruiting such men. Indeed Brennan was one of the very first officials to transfer, in February 1922, when Collins asked his British contacts whether there were any suitable Irishmen working in Dublin Castle who could help him establish the Department of Finance.

Brennan's role looms large in any assessment of the British administrative and governmental legacy of 1922 for a variety of reasons. It was largely due to Brennan, for example, that the 1922 Constitution and, later, the 1937 Constitution 'enshrine what have been called the "fundamental principles" of the British financial system' – principles which in the British case, moreover, rested on usage rather than on special statute. These principles were three: that all money must be got and spent only for that specific purpose to which parliament has appropriated it; that all money must be paid into and out of the same single fund; and that the unit of time for financial administrators was the year and all annual current expenditure must be met out of annual current receipts. The three principles find expression in Articles 37, 61 and 36 and 54 of the 1922 Constitution.

More generally, the Irish system of financial controls was, in all its essential features, the British system. This is not surprising seeing that the period of 120 years from the Act of Union until 1922 coincided, or nearly so, with the most important period of evolution in British financial administration, from the reforms of Pitt down to the Exchequer and Audit Department Act of 1921.[31]

In practice the effective implementation of financial control had been secured months before the enactment of the Constitution on 25 October 1922. On 16 March 1922, for example, a fortnight *before* functions and services were formally transferred by the British, a Finance circular was issued to all other departments laying claim to 'the duties at present performed by the English Treasury' and insisting 'that no proposal involving fresh expenditure of public money should be put into effect' without Finance's 'prior concurrence'.[32]

In many instances Finance silently assumed powers which the Treasury exercised in the United Kingdom without even seeking approval for their so doing. One striking case was a memorandum drafted by Brennan in April 1922 which laid down the procedures to be followed in any department initiating a proposal for additional and unauthorised expenditure. It elicited the inquiry from the Minister for Agriculture, Patrick Hogan, whether the procedure had been already adopted or whether it was merely being proposed for the consideration of the government – other departments, Hogan noted, had not been asked for their observations. Finance's reply was lofty and immediate – by return of post, in fact: 'as the procedure in question is only in accordance with recognised principles of public finance it was not considered necessary to ask for any observations in regard to it'.[33] That seems to have settled the matter for there is no evidence that it was subsequently referred to the government.

One matter which was referred to the government was the appointment of P. S. O'Hegarty 'in charge of the GPO as Acting-Administrator' on 1 February 1922 when it was also agreed that that title would be used generally for such appointments in other offices. By 3 April, however, the Provisional Government minutes had silently slipped into the British usage of 'Secretary' and on 24 April O'Hegarty's appointment 'as Secretary to the GPO was confirmed'.[34] No less remarkable was the fact that the Provisional Government is nowhere earlier recorded as having considered or confirmed the appointment of Secretaries to other government departments. Their translation from the headship of corresponding boards or offices under British rule seems to have been quasi-automatic and taken as read.

The persistence of British nomenclature is also revealed in the continued use of 'Treasury' instead of Department (or Ministry) of Finance. This prevailed until the Provisional Government was replaced by the Executive Council when the Irish Free State came into being on 6 December 1922 and occasional usages of 'Treasury' still surfaced thereafter.[35]

The tendency to follow faithfully in British footsteps was again reflected in the decision to vest the general organisation and regulation of the entire civil service in the Department of Finance. In Britain, wrote one critic of this development, 'the Treasury stands over the civil service administration and there is in this country a desire, even a resolve, to place the Department of Finance in a position corresponding to that of the Treasury in Great Britain'.[36] That resolve was first manifested in a letter of 3 May 1922 which Michael Collins

> had issued to all Ministers advising them that the Ministry of Finance would be responsible for transfers of staff necessitated by the formation of new Departments and the re-organisation of old ones and that the decision of the Secretary to the Treasury in regard to such transfers should be regarded as final;

a letter which Collins formally read to his colleagues at a Provisional Government meeting next day.[37]

The man most responsible for the organisation of the Irish civil service was C. J. Gregg. Although Gregg was an Irishman, who had been a contemporary of Eamon De Valera's at Blackrock College, his earlier civil service career had been in London with the exception of a period when he had served as private secretary to Sir Hamar Greenwood, the much hated Chief Secretary who had presided over the British administration during the most bloody phase of the Anglo-Irish war. It spoke volumes for Collins's indifference to the political ramifications of the British legacy that he should have borrowed Gregg from the British Board of Inland Revenue from April 1922 until October 1924.[38]

One of Gregg's first major tasks was the establishment of a Civil Service Commission in the new state. The episode is of particular interest for the student of the British administrative legacy in as much as it provoked a rare debate about the appropriateness of the British model in Irish circumstances. This debate was occasioned by the report of Dr Henry Kennedy of University College, Dublin who had been invited to make proposals to the government on the recruitment policy for the Irish public service in the future. Kennedy contrasted the British practice of centralising the control of the civil service under the Treasury with the looser and wider control exercised in other British Dominions and in the USA. He recommended that the suitability of 'the system of control which is universal among English speaking peoples outside of Britain be carefully considered'.

Gregg, Brennan and T. K. Bewley (another senior civil servant on loan from London to the Irish government) all reacted strongly against Kennedy's proposed departure from British practice. So, too, did the only ministers who appear to have responded to the invitation of W. T. Cosgrave, issued in his capacity as President of the Executive Council, to submit memoranda on the report – in itself an unusual index of the gravity with which the issues were regarded. J. J. Walsh thought Kennedy's report 'too heavily based upon what Canada or Australia or the United States does' and argued that it was not a time to experiment with schemes which have been born of the experience and the conditions in other countries. The British Civil Service system has operated in this country for the past sixty-years, and *no matter what our views may be on the institutions of Britain generally* (my italics), its Civil Service Commission is without a doubt one of the finest and most impartial institutions of its kind in the world.

Eoin MacNeill agreed and argued that 'the duties of the Civil Service Commission should conform to the excellent model of the British Commission of which, so far as I know, there has been no complaint as to efficiency and suitability'.[39] And conform with the British Commission it duly did. The Civil Service Regulation Act of 1924 was in the same mould. 'You may be interested to see our Civil Service Regulation Act of which I enclose a copy', wrote Gregg to a Treasury official, in London; 'it is practically a reproduction of the British Orders-in-Council'.[40]

Another striking instance of Collins's readiness to institute British administrative practices was contained in a memorandum he forwarded to the Provisional Government shortly after the outbreak of the civil war which listed questions he wanted circulated to all civil servants with a view to demanding a declaration of fidelity to the government. One question ran 'Have you read the Official Secrets Act, and are you prepared loyally to abide by terms of same?'[41] That Act was, of course, the British Official Secrets Act of 1911.

The fact that Collins and Cosgrave both chose to hold the Finance portfolio in addition to the premier place among ministers greatly strengthened their authority and was arguably the single most significant factor in the smooth absorption of the British legacy. Collins's authority among the supporters of the Treaty was paramount and Cosgrave donned that mantle. This happened when he was simultaneously appointed acting chairman of the Provisional Government and acting Minister of Finance on 12 July 1922 due to Collins's absence on military duties as Commander-in-Chief.[42] On 30 August, after Collins's death, Cosgrave assumed both positions on a permanent basis, becoming in addition President of Dáil Éireann on 9 September and, on 6 December, the first President of the Executive Council of the Irish Free State. Not until September 1923 did he finally relinquish the Finance portfolio.

The strength of continuity between Collins and Cosgrave in regard to the British legacy was apparent at the Provisional Government meeting of 12 July 1922 when Cosgrave was appointed acting chairman. He immediately used his newfound authority to emphasise 'the necessity for adhering to the instructions already given to Ministers that no scheme involving expenditure should be proceeded with until it has first been considered and approved by the Treasury [sic]'.[43]

That the Minister of Finance was also Head of Government afforded inestimable advantages to those senior officials who were concerned with the control and regulation of the civil service in their endeavours to root the British legacy in the administrative and governmental foundations of independent Ireland during such seminal years. Nor should one underestimate the influence of the bonding effect between ministers and officials closeted behind the sandbagged defences of Government Buildings in Merrion Street during the most dangerous days of the civil war.

Joe Brennan enjoyed working with Collins who, he recalled, 'accepted advice and gave the go-ahead. He was a vigorous active fellow who would have found finance too dull for a full-time occupation. His mind was full of the problem of the Irregulars and of fighting the civil war.' Brennan also 'found it easy to work with Cosgrave . . . The two men were cautiously conservative in their approach to the spending of public money.' Their system, avowed Brennan, 'was modelled after the British system – a very excellent system . . . (which) would give the best results'.[44]

It was wholly appropriate that it should later fall to Joseph Brennan, writing in 1935 in his capacity as the Chairman of the First Commission of Inquiry into the Civil Service of independent Ireland to pen what has become the classic summary of Britain's administrative and governmental legacy:

The passing of the state services into the control of a native government, however revolutionary it may have been as a step in the political development of the nation, entailed, broadly speaking, no immediate disturbance of any fundamental kind in the daily work of the average civil servant. Under changed masters the same main tasks of administration continued to be performed by the same staffs on the same general lines of organisation and procedure.[45]

And, as I have written elsewhere, what was true of the 1922 change from British to Irish 'masters' was no less true of the only change of Irish masters before 1948 when Fianna Fáil formed their first government in 1932.[46] In 1934 some 10,000 civil servants transferred in 1922 (about 45 per cent of the civil service as a whole) still held office.

The climax of the career of one such civil servant, Owen J. Redmond, who became Secretary of the Department of Finance in 1953 at the age of sixty-three, hammers the point home. Redmond had first entered the public service as a fifteen-year-old boy clerk in the Office of Public Works in 1906, only five years after the death of Queen Victoria, and was one of the first officers who transferred to the Department of Finance in 1922. His climb to 'the last rung on the ladder leading to the highest post in the Irish civil service was a truly remarkable testimony to the endurance of the *ancien régime*'.[47]

What held good of personnel held good of procedure. One example will suffice: the instructions on cabinet procedure which incorporated the principles of financial control and were issued by the Attorney-General in 1924. Reissued in 1930, they were again revised after Fianna Fáil came to power in 1932 when the Department of Finance's effective power of veto over any proposed legislation involving public expenditure was made still more explicit.[48] Nor did the then Secretary of the Department of Finance, Jimmy McElligott, see anything incongruous about circulating Fianna Fáil ministers at the height of the Economic War with a facsimile of a notice issued originally by the Permanent Secretary to the Treasury for the guidance of British ministers. The explicit inclusion of the doctrine of collective cabinet responsibility in both the 1922

Constitution (Article 54) and the 1937 Constitution (Article 28-4-2) similarly shows that De Valera was no more averse to British precedent than Collins and Cosgrave.

Basil Chubb has suggested that, despite the paucity of changes in the structure of Irish government and administration,

> it was not to be expected that so British an organisation would remain for long unaltered in character and attitudes in a country whose social structure and social ideas were always different and became increasingly so after the Treaty. The tone of the British higher civil service, especially the gentlemanly, generalist, clubman, Oxbridge tradition of its senior ranks, could hardly survive in an Irish service which soon became peopled at the top level by officers who, though middle class, were often lower rather than upper middle class.[49]

The point is well made and is borne out by the failure to introduce the Junior Administrative Office class as an elite cadre of university graduates to provide a recruiting reservoir for the highest posts in the civil service. The protests from within the parallel Executive Officer Grade, composed of school-leavers who went straight into the public service, were ferocious and successful. The concept of H. P. Boland, the Establishments Officer in the Department of Finance from 1924 to 1937, that Junior Administrative Officers should be 'a *corps d'elite* – which found expression in private dinner parties which he held for them in the Gresham Hotel – was shattered by the promotions from the executive stream to the Assistant Principal Grade; this contrasted with the British practice'.[50]

The use of the Irish language was another obvious mark of changed character. Michael Collins 'pointed out that it was essential that each department should become thoroughly Irish' as early as May 1922, when he demanded 'that forms, circulars etc. associated with the old administration should be altered to meet the new conditions. The use of the Irish language should be introduced wherever possible'.[51]

Ernest Blythe, who as Minister for Finance was responsible for the control and regulation of the civil service from 1923 until 1932, was one of the most ardent advocates of the language revival which got a further boost with Fianna Fáil's entry to office. Even the Clongowes and Cambridge educated Brennan 'conformed to the practice in the early days of the state of signing his name in Irish, using the antiquated form of Seosamh Ua Braonáin'.[52]

But, for the most part, senior officials merely genuflected in the direction of the native god without losing their faith in the doctrines preached in the temples of Whitehall. One index of the continuing intimacy between Irish and British officials was that their correspondence was sometimes conducted on Christian name terms, which was rare in the correspondence between heads of Irish government departments.[53] Another was the direct telephone line between the Department of Finance and the Treasury throughout the Second World War, the imperatives of Irish neutrality notwithstanding. The line served as a kind of umbilical cord affording mutual nourishment to the mandarins of Whitehall and Merrion Street.

The evidence, in sum, is overwhelming that Irish and British officials alike saw no conflict between the objectives of their respective political masters and the prudent and prolonged expenditure of the legacy bequeathed by Britain to Ireland in 1922–23.

Nor is there any substantial evidence that many of those political masters thought otherwise – Seán MacBride, who argued that most senior officials in the Irish civil service 'are merely British secret service agents',[54] was the exception who proved the rule. One clue to the easy acceptance of the British legacy may lie in the thesis that to Sinn Féin at the advent of independence 'most central government departments were significant more as symbols of authority than as instruments of power'.[55] For, however broad and bitter the divide between William Cosgrave and Eamon De Valera, they shared the common objective of wanting to possess the symbols of authority in the new state. Both saw possession of the British legacy of government and administration not as an end in itself but as a means to an end. That their ends were in conflict – the maintenance of the Treaty in the first case and its destruction in the second – was ultimately irrelevant. As long as that legacy enabled them to achieve their respective political objectives, neither they nor the great majority of their colleagues cared much about the terms of their inheritance.

Acknowledgement: I owe a special debt of gratitude to Maeve Bradley for the speed and efficiency with which she prepared the typescript of this chapter.

REFERENCES

1. Winston S. Churchill, *The Aftermath* (New York, 1929), p. 296.
2. Brian Farrell, *The Founding of Dáil Éireann* (Dublin, 1971), pp. 23–4.
3. See State Paper Office (SPO) DE 2/440.
4. Farrell, *The Founding*, p. 68.
5. Text of constitution as amended on 1 April 1919, SPO DE 2/471.
6. The amended text is printed as Appendix 1 to *Private sessions of Second Dáil* (Dublin, n.d.).
7. SPO DE 1/1–3.
8. Tom Barry, *Guerilla Days in Ireland* (Tralee, 1969), p. 7.
9. *Minutes of Proceedings of the First Dáil*, p. 152; see also pp. 278–9 for the discussion of 11 March 1921.
10. Farrell, *The Founding*, p. 78.
11. See *Minutes of First Dáil*, pp. 213–14; the resolution was proposed by J. J. Walsh.
12. Cf. Ronan Fanning, *The Irish Department of Finance 1922–58* (Dublin, 1978), pp. 15–25 for a fuller account – hereafter cited as Fanning, *Finance*. Much of what follows summarises or amends passages there given at greater length.
13. Fanning, *Finance*, p. 26.
14. SPO DE 2/7.
15. SPO DE 1/3/126.
16. SPO DE 2/9.
17. SPO DE 2/443.
18. Cf. Fanning, *Finance*, pp. 7–8.
19. A. P. Waterfield (head of the Treasury office in Dublin Castle) to the Provisional Government, 23 January 1922, Public Record Office (PRO) (London) T.162/85/E.9478.
20. *Irish Independent*, 19 January 1922.
21. Terence de Vere White, *Kevin O'Higgins* (Tralee, 1966), p. 84.
22. Interview with the author, 24 February 1971.

23. House of Lords Record Office, Lloyd George papers, F 31/1/33, 15 May 1920.
24. See John Wheeler-Bennett, *John Anderson: Viscount Waverly* (London, 1962).
25. John McColgan, *British Policy and the Irish Administration 1920-22* (London, 1983), p. 86.
26. Heads B and C of part 1 of the rules in the 8th schedule.
27. *Report of the Commission of Inquiry into the Civil Service 1932–35* (hereafter cited as *Brennan Report*), p. 1844, Vol. 1, Appendix 3.
28. See T. K. Whitaker, *Interests* (Dublin, 1983), p. 287; also Fanning, *Finance*, pp. 59–60.
29. See Leon Ó Broin, *No Man's Man – a Biographical Memoir of Joseph Brennan* (Dublin, 1982), pp. 97–102; also Fanning, *Finance*, p. 40.
30. See Ó Broin, *op. cit.*, pp. 87–94.
31. See G. P. S. Hogan, 'The constitutional basis of financial control', in *Administration*, VII, 2, p. 158.
32. Hogan, 'The constitutional basis', p. 155.
33. Cf. Fanning, *Finance*, pp. 47–8.
34. SPO, G 1/1/51 and G 1/2/5, 24.
35. See, for example, the Executive Council minutes of 20 December 1922 (SPO, G 2/1) where Brennan is described as 'of the Treasury'. Cf. Fanning, *Finance*, pp. 38–9, for a more detailed discussion of nomenclature.
36. *Brennan Report*, Luke Duffy's minority report, i, p. 148.
37. See SPO G 1/2/29 and S. 2125.
38. See Fanning, *Finance*, pp. 43, 77–80, 642 n.59; also Ó Broin, *No Man's Man*, p. 132.
39. Cf. Fanning, *Finance*, pp. 63–72.
40. *Ibid.*, p. 72.
41. *Ibid.*, p. 55.
42. SPO S. 1.
43. SPO S. 1093.
44. Ó Broin, *No Man's Man*, pp. 115, 119, 125.
45. *Brennan Report*, i, paragraph 8.
46. Cf. Ronan Fanning, *Independent Ireland* (Dublin, 1983), pp. 61–2.
47. Cf. Fanning, *Finance*, p. 493.
48. *Ibid.*, pp. 102–4.
49. Basil Chubb, 'Fifty years of Irish administration' in Owen Dudley Edwards and Fergus Pyle (eds), *1916: the Easter Rising* (London, 1968), p. 187.
50. Fanning, *Finance*, p. 542.
51. Minutes of Provisional Government meeting of 15 May 1922, SPO G 1/2/46.

52. Ó Broin, *No Man's Man*, pp. 110–11.
53. Cf. Fanning, *Finance*, p. 433.
54. National Library of Ireland, MS 17456; 19 October 1932.
55. McColgan, *British Policy and the Irish Administration*, p. 70.

4 · Britain's legacy to the Irish social security system

GEOFFREY COOK

This chapter seeks to assess the influence of British social security policy on Irish social security policy. First, there is a review of the British legacy which Ireland inherited at the time of political independence. Secondly there is a discussion of the separate developments of social security policy in Britain and in independent Ireland. These developments are related to a three-stage model of socio-economic development and the impact of unemployment. The influence of the Beveridge Report and the reforms of the post-war Labour government are assessed in relation to Irish developments. Lastly, there is a review of recent changes in social security policy in both countries and an assessment of the changing relationships between the two countries' social security policies.

The origins of the modern social security system in Britain and Ireland lie in the reformed Poor Law of 1834 in Britain. 'Deterrence', the 'workhouse test', and 'less eligibility' became the principal operative principles of the 1838 Poor Law in Ireland in a society which had not hitherto been subject to a comprehensive Poor Law.[1] Thus, the Irish Poor Law was explicitly modelled on the British reformed Poor Law and legislation aimed at tackling destitution and vagrancy in the rapidly industrialising society of Britain was applied to the overwhelmingly rural and subsistence agriculture society of Ireland. The principle of deterrence was fundamental and the objective of social control explicit. Only those most in need of poor relief were to be recipients of the Poor Law, and the test of whom was to receive benefit was submission to the workhouse test, whereby all relief for the able-bodied was to be discharged in a workhouse. The level of relief was to be such that an applicant for relief was rendered 'less eligible' than an independent (i.e. self-supporting) day labourer. This principle of less eligibility linked to the workhouse test was particularly attractive to the utilitarian Poor Law reformers because it was self-actualising, i.e. the applicant for relief decided whether he or she could withstand the ignominy of the workhouse test and the degrading life in the workhouse thereafter. Extensive bureaucracy established to determine desert was avoided by the self-actualising operation of the deterrent principles of the Poor Law. Only the most necessitous and destitute would seek relief because the terms on which relief was to be distributed were so brutal.

The pristine terms on which the Poor Law was supposed to operate were virtually completely abrogated by the experience of the Great Famine of the late 1840s. The famine experience in Ireland showed the total inability of the Poor Law to cope with mass destitution, starvation and death. After the abatement of famine conditions, considerable attempts were made to restore the deterrent principle and less eligibility. In so far as these attempts were successful, emigration from Ireland was facilitated, despite the operation of settlement laws in Britain to return the poor of a Poor Law Union to the union from which they originally came.

Major reforms in social security policy came not so much with the total breakdown of the Poor Law in the wake of the famine, but half a century later with the growth of the trade union movement and socialist parties and the growing acceptance that the Poor Law principles were not the best means of responding to the causes of dependency in an industrialising society. Social learning took the form of British reforms applied often without significant modification to the Irish scene, rather than Irish reforms achieved in the wake of Irish evidence and generalised to the whole of Britain as well. The causes of dependency in an industrial society were increasingly identified, responsibility for action often bitterly contested, and when responsibility was resolved the legislative framework for Britain became the framework for legislation in Ireland also. Thus, the Poor Law in Ireland was relatively unreformed but categories of deserving or necessitous personnel were removed from the aegis of the Poor Law and categorical provision was made. The first formal break with the Poor Law came after the introduction of the bitterly contested Workmens' Compensation Act of 1897. This Act placed liability on employers to pay compensation in respect of death or injury of a workman from an accident arising out of and in the course of employment. Both the range of employments and the amount of compensation were limited, but the break with the Poor Law had been made. The second break with the Poor Law was the introduction of Old Age Pensions in 1908, again covering both Britain and Ireland. The pension was means-tested and only provided after stern character, nationality and age tests had also been passed. The third break with the Poor Law came with the introduction of 'national insurance for sickness and unemployment' for certain categories of workers in 1911, a generation after social insurance had been pioneered by Bismarck in the German Second Reich. *Prima facie*, Ireland appeared to benefit from legislation introduced to benefit British workers.

In order to examine the British legacy of social security in Ireland, various stages of the policy-making process may be discerned. First there is the concept of parallel introduction, that is legislative reform which reformed social security provision in the whole of Britain and Ireland or a separate Irish Act that was introduced at the same time as the British Act. Second, there is the concept of parallel provision which is that legislative provision for Ireland was modelled precisely on provision for Britain. The third stage is parallel implementation in which the legislation is simultaneously enacted and enforced in both countries. Lastly there is the issue of parallel outcome, whereby the question posed is to what extent do similarities in the early stages of the policy process produce a parallel outcome in the two countries concerned?

The parallel introduction and provision of the Workmen's Compensation Act 1897 was not matched by a parallel outcome because the Irish occupational structure outside Belfast and Dublin was much more based on rural occupations and self-employment, compared with the British occupational structure.[2] The parallel introduction and provision of the Old Age Pension Act of 1908 also produced a highly differentiated outcome because there was found to be a much higher proportion of eligible pensioners in Ireland (particularly in the western seabord and the so-called Congested Districts) than in Britain.[3] The Old Age Pension Act of 1908 represents the beginning of a positive redistribution from Britain to Ireland. National insurance in Britain and Ireland had neither parallel provision nor parallel outcome. The National Insurance Act of 1911 sought to provide compulsory national insurance benefits for the contingencies of sickness and unemployment for certain groups of employees with the cost of the scheme met by contributions from the employer, the employee, and the State. While the British scheme included provision of medical care for employees, Ireland was excluded from the medical scheme owing to a successful lobby by the Irish medical profession on the ostensible grounds that the full adoption of the Act in Ireland would restrict the well-established dispensary doctor system.[4]

Thus, the Poor Law, Workmen's Compensation, Old Age Pensions, National Insurance Act for sickness and unemployment, and in 1920 the Blind Pension Act represent the statutory legislative framework for social security inherited by the Irish Free State on the attainment of political independence in 1922. Yet, despite political independence, the British influence on Ireland was still strong. A shared language and media as well as a common labour market and often the same or similar trade unions helped to ensure that despite the intentions of the founders of the Free State, developments in British social security had direct and indirect ramifications in Ireland. Thus priorities for reform in Britain often became transmitted by osmosis through the trade union movement and the media into a similar but not necessarily the same demand for action in Ireland, and

Britain remained the prime social security comparative reference group (not least because Northern Ireland received British social security levels).

The inter-war period was dominated by the spectre of mass unemployment. Politicians and administrators in both countries spent a great deal of time and energy trying to resolve the puzzle of ways of coping with the growing numbers of insured claimants who had exhausted their rights to unemployment benefit. In Britain coverage for unemployment insurance was incrementally extended in the inter-war period to broader categories of the workforce, and several acts sought to make provision for those who had exhausted their rights to unemployment insurance by the payment of 'uncovenanted' and later 'transitional' payments, so that the unemployed would not have to face the degradation of the Poor Law.[5]

In Britain, the series of incremental reforms in unemployment insurance and in reviews of the system culminated in the 1934 Unemployment Act which created the Unemployment Assistance Board with responsibility for the means-testing of claimants for unemployment assistance.[6] In Ireland, the incoming De Valera government in 1932 had promised social action on a broad front. The Unemployment Assistance Act of 1934 was ostensibly designed to meet indigenous conditions and sought to cover all men and some women whether or not they had been covered for unemployment insurance. The Irish Unemployment Assistance Act represented the first piece of legislation to relieve the destitution of the unemployed agricultural worker and save him from recourse to the Poor Law. The hybrid purpose of the legislation to meet the needs of both urban and rural workers caused the scheme to be operated quite differently in rural and urban areas. The complexity of the operation of the legislation with its new appeals procedures rapidly produced a chaotic situation with an unexpectedly high number of applications for assistance. Although the legislation was welcomed by many smallholders, the omnibus character of the provisions of the Act effectively dodged one of Ireland's critical problems: to devise an effective support system for Ireland's marginal farmers, to raise farm productivity, and where necessary to encourage transfers from farming to alternative occupations.

Another political puzzle with which both British and Irish governments wrestled in the inter-war years was the provision for widows and orphans, which was a problem which had been greatly highlighted by the staggering loss of life in the First World War, creating significant dependency effects. The Chamberlain Act of 1925 in Britain sought to extend the health insurance scheme to cover widows' pensions, payable on the husband's contributions with additional allowances for children.[7] Orphans' pensions were to be paid to guardians for orphaned children of insured people, and also the Chamberlain Act included contributory old-age pensions, paid to men from sixty-five, and to women from the age of sixty. Provision was also made for those not compulsorily insured under the health insurance scheme to make voluntary contributions. In Ireland, a Committee of Enquiry under the chairmanship of Joseph Glynn was established 'to enquire and report as to a scheme of widows and orphans pensions suitable to Saorstat Éireann'.[8] The Glynn Committee's Report of 1933 considered that the major question before them was whether a scheme for widows and orphans pensions should be one of contributory insurance or whether any other principles should be applied. The Glynn Committee took full cognisance of the operation of the Chamberlain Act in Britain and reviewed the strengths and weaknesses of workmen's compensation, social insurance and social assistance as methods of social security provision for widows and orphans.

The Glynn Committee effectively divided into two groups producing a Majority and a Minority Report. While the Majority Report favoured a non-contributory (i.e. means-tested) widows and orphans pension scheme, the Minority Report favoured a scheme based on social insurance. Thus the Minority Report's recommendations were much closer to following recent British experience. To resolve the dilemma, the new Fianna Fáil administration under De Valera decided to introduce two schemes. The first scheme was a contributory scheme, whose coverage was to be the same for national health insurance as well as including all public servants, while the second scheme was a means-tested scheme with relatively strict eligibility conditions relating to the widows of persons who would have been insured for contributory pensions when the Act came into operation but whose spouses were already dead, retired or insufficiently insured. The only other group deemed to qualify for the social assistance scheme were the survivors of smallholders. This special concession to those who often lived along the western seaboard of Ireland was abolished two years later when the assistance scheme for widows and orphans was extended to all groups subject to a means test. Thus, in the case of social security for widows and orphans, Ireland partly followed the strategy developed in Britain and partly developed a means-tested strategy. In the case of contributory old-age pensions, however, there was a wide and growing gap between British and Irish provision. In Britain, those covered for health insurance became eligible for contributory old-age pensions, while Ireland relied on the 1908 means-tested scheme, and private and voluntary arrangements for support in old age.

This duality of social security responses, i.e. following British developments in certain instances and making indigenous developments in Irish social security on other occasions continued in the later years of Fianna Fáil rule. The Public Assistance Act of 1939 removed the title but not the spirit of the Poor Law from Irish legislation. The local authorities in Ireland became the public assistance authorities offering assistance of last resort called home assistance. This Act implemented some of the proposals of the O'Connor Committee on the relief of the sick and destitute poor, but in some respects the indirect influence of the British Public Assistance Act of 1929 remained apparent at least in terms of administrative rearrangements for public assistance responsibilities.[9] The passage of the Insurance (Intermittent Unemployment) Act of 1942 in Ireland (popularly known as the Wet Time Act) shows the continuance of the developing tradition of attempting to tackle social security problems by indigenous means. The Wet Time Act sought to provide insurance against loss of wages due to bad weather for manual workers in certain outdoor occupations.

In terms of the number of new schemes developed, the early De Valera administration counts as one of the most innovative in the area of social security. To streamline the legacy of approved societies inherited from the British health insurance legislation the Fianna Fáil government decided to integrate all the schemes into one omnibus society, the National Health Insurance Society. This reform gave Ireland a more standardised structure for health insurance than existed in Britain, with its motley collection of approved societies, some offering generous payments and others parsimonious payment levels. The last significant development of this era was the expansion of benefits in kind in Ireland and these ranged from free footwear to free peat schemes. The apparent popularity of such categorically earmarked social security schemes in Ireland compared with Britain has been reinforced over the years with the continued expansion in the number of such schemes. Such expansion has made for great complexity both in administration and in application for such benefits.

In comparing the development of the British and Irish social security systems, the patterns of provision may be related to three stages in a country's socio-economic development. The first stage is when the country is beginning to move from a rural subsistence economy to a society with a rudimentary industrial base. As Gaston Rimlinger has shown, a very variegated pattern of factors, including the philosophy of state action, influence the inauguration of a national social security scheme.[10] The next stage is one of transition from an agriculturally based society to an industrial one in which a nascent social security system can assist in integrating the workforce to the new industrial system. The third stage is one of advanced industrial capitalism with an element of de-industrialisation, great technological advance and in its wake great obsolescence of skill and craft, creating new work and leisure patterns, and a renewed emphasis on social protection and adequate social security. A *priori*, the factors which facilitate the establishment of a social security system are not necessarily the same factors which play an important part in the growth of the system or in the third stage of development. Many states suffered a long time in the second stage of development with only a rudimentary local Poor Law network of provision and no national social security. Thus, Britain did not advance from Poor Law social security till 1897 (Workmen's Compensation), 1908 (Old Age Pensions) and 1911 (National Insurance) which included the pioneering of unemployment insurance. This heritage formed the basis of the Irish system at independence when in terms of economic and social development, the Republic was at stage one. In this respect, the Republic possessed a head start in social protection. As Britain and Ireland started in harness it is interesting to compare social security expenditure as a proportion of GNP in each country with their own separate developments. Thus, in 1976 the British proportion was 10.4 per cent while the Irish was 10.5 per cent; in 1981 these proportions were 10.6 and 10.7 per cent respectively, endorsing Aaron's finding that the single most important variable explaining the size of the social security budget is the length of time a social security system has been in operation.[11]

The role that unemployment has played in the growth and development of Britain's and Ireland's social security systems has been a vital one. Briggs writing about British social policy is unequivocal: 'Unemployment is a product of industrial societies and it is unemployment more than any other social contingency which has determined the shape and timing of modern social welfare legislation'.[12] The importance of unemployment as a factor in social security development must be related to the three stage model of socio-economic development. The unemployment created by the dislocation of a subsistence economy when it begins to build an industrial base raises general concern for the need for the redeployment of the labour force. Yet unemployment compensation schemes rarely arise among the first developments of national social security. In the case of Britain and Ireland, unemployment was not a prime mover in the first national social security schemes, but the national insurance schemes of 1911 did include the pioneer development of a restricted and residual scheme of unemployment insurance, which was later emulated around the world. Unemployment and redundancy schemes came to play a much bigger part in social security provisions in the second and third stages of the model of socio-economic development. As eligibility for unemployment compensation broadens and deepens and self-employment contracts, social security expenditure for the unemployed becomes an important stabilising transfer payment and plays a crucial latent role in reducing potential militancy about the socio-economic system amongst the beneficiaries.

The direct and indirect impacts of the British social security system on the Irish system were clearly shown during and after the Second World War, when the Beveridge Report was published in Britain and widely debated and the post-war Labour Government attempted to implement the spirit if not the letter of the Report.[13] Published in the middle of the Second World War, the Beveridge Report had in fact been a best-seller. To the war-torn troops and to the blitz-damaged civilians, it provided both a rationale for winning the war and a framework for social reconstruction that would mean the cessation of hostilities would not bring about the return of mass unemployment, the degradation of dole queues and the Poor Law. The Report itself focused on the extension of coverage of social insurance and the payment of flat-rate benefits for flat-rate contributions. The comprehensiveness of coverage was one of the most important aspects of the Report's recommendations. All members of the population and not merely the employed were to be covered for all major social risks. Beveridge clearly saw that the extension and implementation of the social insurance system would not be an adequate protection against the return of pre-war conditions in Britain. Indeed he viewed his social insurance reforms against a background of other vitally necessary reforms which included the creation of a National Health Service, the introduction of family allowances and above all the commitment by government as an over-riding priority to full employment.

Although the Coalition Government gave this commitment and endorsed the ideals of the Beveridge Report, the post-war Labour government had the responsibility for implementing the structural reforms. The 1946 National Insurance Act extended compulsory insurance to all members of the population of working age, and categorised them into employed people, self-employed people, married women and non-earners. Under the National Insurance (Industrial Injuries) Act of 1946, the Workmen's Compensation Scheme was replaced by a national insurance scheme for industrial accidents and diseases. For those who fell through the net of social insurance, the Labour government provided a scheme of national assistance (means-tested). Family allowances were introduced, a very popular National Health Service was created among many other reforms, which *in toto* created what became known as the British Welfare State.

Against this background of major social reconstruction in Britain, based on widening state responsibilities, Bishop John Dignan in Ireland issued a monograph on social security which sought to remove the taint of pauperism, destitution and degradation from the social security and health services.[14] The Dignan Plan proposed to extend the role of the National Health Insurance Society by the provision of enhanced sickness, disability, marriage and maternity benefits and by the provision of completely new retirement and death benefits. In comparison with the flat-rate benefits proposed and implemented in Britain, Dignan proposed income-related contributions and income-related benefits, with the proposed sickness benefit set at approximately half the average weekly wage and the disability benefit set at about one-third or one-quarter of the average weekly wage.

Dignan proposed that membership of the enlarged National Health Insurance Society was to be compulsory for all employed people irrespective of income, while the self-employed were to be allowed to become voluntary contributors. One important feature of the scheme was that the management was to be based on vocational principles (i.e. by occupation). In fact the Dignan scheme was devised to pre-empt demands for a greatly extended and rationalised state social security and medical service, as envisaged in the Beveridge Report in Britain.

The fall of the De Valera administration and the coming to power of the Costello Inter-party Government in 1948 provided the impetus for a re-evaluation of social security policy and the publication of the 1949 White Paper on Social Security, the only such document ever issued in the history of the independent Irish state.[15] The White Paper proposed that compulsory coverage for social insurance would be restricted to all employed people (similar to the Dignan proposals which also allowed for voluntary contributions from the self-employed). The range of contingencies to be covered extended beyond ill-health, unemployment, and maternity to include retirement and death. The wider range of social risks to be covered in the proposed reform shows the influence of both the Beveridge and the Dignan Reports but the fact that the state rather than a vocationally organised society was to be the organ of administration suggests the influence of the Beveridge Report. The principle of flat-rate contribution for flat-rate benefits (except for low paid workers) shows the predominance of the Beveridge principles in comparison to the earnings-related proposals of the Dignan Report and the practice of several other European countries. The publication of the White Paper produced a torrent of vituperative criticism, which only abated with the fall of the Costello Government over the Mother and Child proposals.[16]

The incoming De Valera government introduced the 1952 Social Welfare Act which was a truncated version of the previous Government's social security proposals. Coverage for social insurance was limited to employees earning beneath a certain income ceiling, while death grants and contributory retirement pensions were axed altogether. Although enacted this way for reasons of economic stringency, the 1952 Social

Welfare Act clearly reflected a subsidiary role for government in line with the Roman Catholic Church's theory of subsidiarity. In terms of benefit levels, contingencies covered and proportions of the community offered social protection, the 1952 Social Welfare Act was both residual and parsimonious. The influence of the Beveridge Report on the Social Welfare Act of 1952 may be judged therefore to be marginal. The main yet weak influences may be said to be an element of administrative rationalisation and the Irish adoption of the principles of flat-rate contributions and flat-rate benefits. Even in this case, administrative expediency rather than commitment to the flat-rate principle was the rationale as flat-rate contributions and benefits were judged easier to collect and to administer. The net result of these reforms was that a significant proportion of the workforce, the self-employed and many higher paid employees, were not covered for social insurance and thus became reliant on social assistance at a time of dependency. Irish expenditure on social security had thus a much higher proportion spent on means-tested social assistance in comparison with Britain and other European countries which extended their social insurance programmes. This continued heavy reliance on social assistance in Ireland may be regarded as the antithesis of the Beveridge ideology in which the extension of social insurance would reduce social assistance to a negligible role.

In Britain the rising level of post-war consumer affluence generated by the relatively successful pursuit of full employment policies helped to produce a reassessment of social support for dependency and a reconceptualisation of the meaning of poverty. One of the biggest changes from the Beveridge approach to social security came with the introduction of earnings-related benefits and contributions. From 1966, earnings-related supplements were paid to supplement unemployment, sickness and maternity benefit, and short-term widows benefit. The responsibilities of the private and public sectors for the payment of earnings-related retirement pensions took a very long time to resolve through the political system, with the Labour governments pressing for major state responsibility for earnings-related pensions and Conservative governments pressing for a much more extended role for private occupational pension schemes to top up the basic state pension.

In order to reduce the stigma of the National Assistance Scheme and to emphasise the right to receive social security when dependent, the National Assistance scheme in Britain was replaced by the Supplementary Benefit scheme. The creation of Supplementary Benefit was an attempt to make means-testing more acceptable to applicants for assistance and to enhance take-up.[17] This strategy had mixed success among the diverse claimant population.

In post-war Ireland, the appreciable rise in living standards associated with the consumer boom arrived later than in many other countries. The rise in Gross National Product per head did facilitate an expansion of the social security programmes. The highly categorical system of social insurance became even more highly categorised, as successive insurance benefits were added to the framework provided by the 1952 Social Welfare Act. Thus, over a period of years, contributory old-age pensions, death grants, invalidity pensions, retirement pensions and deserted wives' benefit were added. In a similar way, various new categories of social assistance were developed: assistance for unmarried mothers, deserted wives, prisoners' wives, and single women aged over fifty-eight, as well as assistance schemes for disabled people. Thus, both the Irish social insurance and social assistance systems became extremely complex. The identification of the appropriate benefit and separate claims procedures often made the establishment of welfare rights difficult, particularly when certain schemes were stigmatising to claimants, and the visibility and cause of claimant status were reinforced by the categorical nature of the system.

The political puzzle over the future of certain Irish social security schemes was continued in the post-war era by the establishment of committees of enquiry to review policy options. The seven-year review (1955–62) of the Workmen's Compensation scheme produced both a Majority and a

Minority Report.[18] The Majority Report favoured the retention of the system of workmen's compensation while the Minority Report recommended the adoption of an occupational injuries scheme as part of categorical social insurance as adopted in Britain and Northern Ireland. The Minority Report found that the Workmen's Compensation scheme was complex and unwieldy, and left too much scope for contention between the workman and his employer or his employer's insurance company. The duality of responses witnessed in the reform of other social security programmes thus re-emerged again, i.e. to follow the British path or to adopt an alternative strategy, in this case to maintain the status quo. The debate was resolved when the Fianna Fáil administration under Seán Lemass resolved to implement the Minority Report's recommendations and follow the British structure by the development of an Occupational Injuries scheme under social insurance, eighteen years after the establishment of the British scheme.

Not all social security reforms in Ireland came with a long time lag after reform in Britain or involved an identical social security response. In the wake of the Anglo-Irish free trade agreement of 1965 and a reinforcement of the common labour market links between Britain and Ireland, both countries' legislatures passed Redundancy Payment Acts that sought to compensate workers who had lost their jobs on account of redundancy. While the British legislation gave the redundant person a lump sum related to the length of service with his or her employer, the Irish legislation gave the redundant worker a lump sum and a weekly payment. While the lump sum given in Ireland was related to the worker's length of service and his or her normal earnings prior to redundancy, the weekly payment was contingent on unemployment and was to be paid out of a special fund to be financed by contributions from employers and employees. The weekly payment system was in lieu of an earnings-related payment system (which had been introduced to cover the contingency of unemployment in Britain). When a few years later the weekly payment system was abolished, the

Irish redundancy payments system had a much closer resemblance to the British scheme.

Earnings-related payments in addition to the basic social insurance payment levels were introduced in Ireland in 1974 for the contingencies of unemployment, sickness and maternity. The benefits were funded by earnings-related contributions, and the income ceiling on employees' participation in the Social Insurance scheme was abolished. The contingencies for which earnings-related payments were paid were similar in both Britain and Ireland (although Britain had an earnings-related short-term widows' allowance which Ireland did not follow). The perceived short-term nature of the contingencies chosen for earnings-related payments and the neglect of earnings-related payments for the longer term causes of dependency reveals the importance of trade union influence, the common labour market link between the two countries, and the desire of the two governments to contain costs and to target the benefits on workers who would rapidly return to the labour market.

While in some cases, Irish emulation of British initiatives in social security reform were beneficial to the appropriate target groups and had a clear rationale, in other cases the imitative Irish programme lacked relevance or even coherence. The Supplementary Welfare Allowance Act of 1975 in Ireland abolished the provisions of the 1939 Public Assistance Act, and established means-tested supplementary welfare allowances as a means-tested service of last resort to be administered by health boards and not the Department of Social Welfare. This legislation was closely modelled on the Supplementary Benefits Act of 1966 in Britain but lacked the coherence of the British legislation because it represented one further means-tested categorical assistance scheme added to a whole host of existing schemes rather than the integration of the assistance schemes. In short the problems of multiple means-testing were ignored in Ireland with direct deleterious effects on take-up rates and poverty traps. One means-tested benefit – Family Income Supplement – was introduced in Ireland in 1985, fifteen years after the British scheme.

The demise of the Irish scheme was announced along with its creation, so that take-up rates were guaranteed to be low. The rationale for its brief appearance was that the whole area of family income support was to be reformed.[19] Ireland had in fact introduced a scheme of children's allowances in 1944, one year before Britain, but although eligibility had been extended to include all children, the Irish scheme was the least generous in real terms in western Europe. With the demise of the Family Income Supplement in Ireland, the new child benefit became payable from 1986. Again the model for the reform had been the abolition of child tax allowances and family allowances in Britain in 1977 and the payment of integrated child benefit payable to the mother.

As well as the direct British influence on social security policy in Ireland, Ireland's membership of various international organisations like the Organisation for Economic Cooperation and Development, the International Labour Organisation and the International Social Security Association have helped to broaden horizons and to focus discussions on floors of social security provision and improved communication flows. Of decisive significance was Ireland's entry (along with the UK and Denmark) into the European Economic Community. With the EEC's long-term goal of upward harmonisation of social security standards, if not the integration of social security systems, in the short- and medium-term, EEC membership has resulted in a comparison of social security provisions in other member states and Ireland. In this way, reference groups have been widened from the previous UK – Ireland framework or Ireland North and South comparison to a broader European perspective. Of direct consequence to Irish social security policy has been the EEC's concern to improve the entitlements of migrant workers and latterly to oversee the implementation of the EEC's Directive on equal treatment between the sexes in social security policy. Ireland has so far been a laggard in implementing this equal treatment Directive.

The relationship between British and Irish social security policy has undergone a significant change in the 1980s. The Thatcherite axe has fallen on social security expenditure in Britain as social security represents one of the largest single items of government expenditure.[20] The Thatcher Government in Britain has radically overhauled the system and much more retrenchment is planned. Earnings-related benefits have been abolished, and employers have been given the responsibility for the administration if not the finance of short- and medium-term sickness benefit, now called statutory sick pay. Benefits for the disabled have been restructured as has the occupational injuries scheme, while the supplementary benefit has been remodelled with the objective of standardising payments and radically reducing the role of discretionary payments. The re-election of the Thatcher administration in 1983 enhanced the desire for even more radical reforms. Norman Fowler, the Secretary of State for Health and Social Security, established a series of reviews on various areas of social security, which culminated in the publication of the 'Green Papers' – *The Reform of Social Security* – and a White Paper on the future of social security policy.[21] Under these proposals, the role of the State Earnings-related Pension Scheme would be greatly reduced and the Supplementary Benefit Scheme would be replaced by a system of income support for people in clearly defined categories. Those people requiring further means-tested support would be obliged to apply to a cash-limited Social fund. If no assistance could be obtained from such an agency, dependent people would be obliged to turn to charities and relatives and friends for support. The much-vaunted Thatcherite support for Victorian moral values of self-reliance, thrift and unencumbered private enterprise embrace as a corollary a residual role for the state and a late-twentieth-century law for the poor to deter dependency.

Although there have been economies made in social security policy in Ireland, one of the most significant features has been that retrenchment has been marginal not wholesale. Thus, the earnings-related payments have been pruned and certain benefits like Wet Time Insurance have been abolished. The Irish government awaits the publication some time in 1986 of the Report of the Social Welfare Commission, established in 1983 to review the operation of the whole social security system and the Commission may recommend a significant increase in expenditure. The Thatcherite path is of course one option which may gain credibility in Ireland, particularly with the foundation in 1985 of the Progressive Democrats party with an explicit 'roll back the State' ideology. By the mid-1980s, however, there were several contingencies in the social insurance system in which Irish provisions were relatively more generous than British provision for short-term dependencies, e.g. sickness benefit, unemployment benefit, maternity benefit, and occupational injuries benefits. The next few years will show to what extent the British emulation effect dominates over the indigenous reform effect in Irish social security policy.

The British influence on Irish social security policy may be viewed in relation to the three-stage model of socio-economic development discussed earlier. Ireland's inheritance from Britain before political independence included the principal strategies of the Poor Law, social assistance, and finally social insurance. These foundations were laid before Ireland went through stage one, i.e. the transition from a rural subsistence economy to a rudimentary industry society. While Ireland went through stage one and then stage two, the transition from an agriculturally based society to an industrially based society, Britain was a dominant but not determining influence on Irish social security policy. A shared language, media influence, a common labour market and often similar trade unions facilitated this British influence on Irish social security policy, as well as the provision of British benefit structures and levels in Northern Ireland. While Britain went through the third stage of advanced industrial capitalism and some de-industrialisation with a retrenchment of social security structures, Ireland has experienced some de-industrialisation but has not yet followed the Thatcherite path in social security policy.

REFERENCES

1. G. Nicholls, *A History of the Irish Poor Law* (London, 1856). See also S. Ó Cinnéide, *A Law for the Poor* (Dublin, 1970).
2. A. Wilson and H. Levy, *Workman's Compensation* (Oxford, 1946).
3. See P. Thane, unpublished PhD thesis, University of London, 1970.
4. See R. Barrington, unpublished PhD thesis, University of London, 1986.
5. F. Tillyard, *Unemployment Insurance in Great Britain 1911–1948*, (Hadleigh, Essex, 1949).
6. A. Deacon and J. Bradshaw, *Reserved For the Poor* (Oxford, 1983), p. 22.
7. H. Levy, *National Health Insurance*, National Institute of Economic and Social Research, (London, 1944).
8. Saorstát Éireann, *Report of the Committee of Inquiry into Widows and Orphans Pensions*, Chairman Joseph Glynn, R49/1, Stationery Office (Dublin, 1933), p. 103.
9. Saorstát Éireann, *Report of the Commission on the Relief of the Sick and Destitute Poor, including the Insane Poor*, R27/3, Stationery Office (Dublin, 1927).
10. G. Rimlinger, *Welfare Policy and Industrialisation in Europe, America and Russia* (New York, 1971), p. 3.
11. H. Aaron, 'Social security: international comparisons' in O. Eckstein (ed.) *Studies in the Economics of Income Maintenance* (New York, 1967), pp. 13–48.
12. A. Briggs, 'The welfare state in historical perspective', *Archives de Europeannes de Sociologie*, 1961, p. 70. See also Jens Albar 'Government responses to the challenge of unemployment: the development of unemployment insurance in western Europe' in Peter Flora and Arnold Heidenheimer (eds), *The Development of Welfare States in Europe and America*, (New York, 1981), pp. 151–183.
13. *Social Insurance and Allied Services; The Beveridge Report*, Cmd 6404, HMSO (London, 1942).
14. J. Dignan, *Social Security* (Sligo, 1945).
15. White Paper, *Social Security*, Pr.9661, Stationery Office (Dublin 1949).
16. See J. Whyte, *Church and State in Modern Ireland* (Dublin, 1980), 2nd edn.
17. See P. Hall, H. Land, R. Parker and A. Webb, *Change, Choice, and Conflict in Social Policy* (London, 1975).
18. *Commission on Workman's Compensation*, Pr. 6525, Stationery Office (Dublin, 1963).

19. National Economic and Social Council, *Family Income Support*, Stationery Office (Dublin, 1978).
20. D. Bull and P. Wilding (eds), *Thatcherism and the Poor*, Child Poverty Action Group (London, 1983).
21. Green Papers: *The Reform of Social Security*, Cmnd 9517–9519, HMSO (London, 1985) and a White Paper, *The Reform of Social Security*, Cmnd 9691, HMSO (London, 1985).

5 · Anglo-Irish economic interdependence: from excessive intimacy to a wider embrace

DERMOT McALEESE

When Independence came, the Irish economy had been fully integrated with the British economy for roughly a century. Free trade had prevailed since 1820 and monetary unification since 1826. Movements of capital and labour between the islands were unimpeded by restrictions on freedom of access or establishment. A condition of genuine market unification existed. Anglo-Irish trade flows were free from the myriad of frustrating and ingenious non-tariff barriers to trade against which the EEC Commission has struggled in recent years as part of its efforts to create a unified market in the Community.

The consequence of this market unification was, almost inevitably, a heavy dependence on the British market. As Table 5.1 shows Irish exporters sold 84 per cent of their sales to Britain (and most of the remainder to Northern Ireland). Three-quarters of Irish imports came from the UK.[1] There was a strong British presence in Irish industry and in the economic management of the country. In turn, Ireland was an important customer for Britain. We were therefore close economic partners, but Britain was clearly the richer, more powerful and more populated of the two.

Reactions to the consequences of Ireland's integration and dependence differed along predictable lines. The classical economic arguments, drawing on the theory of comparative advantage, pointed to the potential gains from free trade untrammelled by bureaucratic and chauvinistic intervention. This theoretical framework, which is familiar to every first-year student of economics, and the free-trade conclusions customarily derived from it, are not affected by the possibility of one country being larger in size, richer and more

Table 5.1. *Anglo-Irish trade, 1926–84*

	1926	1936	1960	1984
Republic Imports (£m current)	61.3	39.9	226.2	8912.9
% from N. Ireland	10.6	1.4	3.3	3.8
% from Britain	65.1	51.9	46.3	39.1
	75.7	53.3	49.6	42.9
Exports from Republic (£m current)	42.0	22.5	142.7	8897.6
% to N. Ireland	13.6	10.0	13.3	6.6
% to Britain	82.7	81.4	60.4	27.8
	96.3	91.4	73.7	34.4

Note: Pre-1935 import figures are not strictly comparable with later statistics since the former were classified by country of assignment rather than by country of origin.
Source: McAleese Ref. 1, (1977); *Trade Statistics of Ireland*, December 1984.

productive in an absolute sense in all industries than another country. The poorer country may have an absolute disadvantage in all products and still gain substantially through trade by exporting those products in which its *comparative* disadvantage is least. Small size only strengthened the free-trade case since the small country could export without turning the terms of trade against it. Exposure of its import-competing industries to foreign competition would prevent domestic monopolies from abusing their market dominance. Friederich List, who is better known as a protectionist than a free trader, referred to the Anglo-Irish union as 'a great and irrefragable example of the efficiency of free trade between united nations'.[2]

The opposing view, espoused by the nationalists, was critical of Ireland's dependence on Britain, of the country's failure to develop industrially and of the fiscal arrangements applied to Ireland. The economic arguments in favour of political independence were regarded as of subsidiary importance in the build-up of nationalist sentiment. They were not therefore very well articulated and were not subject to much debate in the period immediately preceding independence. Nevertheless, the hypothesis that Ireland could perform better economically and sustain a larger population if Britain allowed her to do so had a long pedigree in Irish history. Henry Grattan at the end of the eighteenth century had argued the need for an independent commercial policy to protect Irish industry against the competitive advantage of British factories. The call for protection was renewed at various stages in the nineteenth century, notably by Isaac Butt and the Home Rule campaign, and was built into the programme of Sinn Féin.

Thus in 1922 the fact of integration was confronted by a strong body of sentiment, buttressed by flimsy but suggestive economic reasoning, advocating a policy of economic independence or economic disintegration between the two islands. There were two strong forces opposing this sentiment. First, some Irish industrialists, who were dependent on export markets and exposed to the threat of retaliation, had no interest in policies of disintegration. Secondly, farmers in both parts of Ireland were dependent on Britain as an outlet for exports and were conscious of the dangers of a policy of economic self-sufficiency. The first group were located primarily in Northern Ireland and as Partition became more solidly entrenched in the 1920s, the Northern interest became gradually more irrelevant. The weakening of world agricultural markets in the late 1920s, and the diminished outlets for emigration from many areas of rural Ireland which resulted from the Great Depression greatly weakened the force of the agricultural anti-protection lobby. These two factors, together with the increased stabilisation of the country's finances during the 1920s, opened the way for an Irish government to implement the type of economic policies which nationalist rhetoric had demanded for so long and from which so much had been promised.[3]

THE ERA OF PROTECTION

Fianna Fáil came to power in 1932 on the basis of a firm commitment to protectionist policies. There were three aspects of these policies which had a particular bearing on Anglo-Irish economic relations: industrial protectionism, control of foreign investment and encouragement of tillage. The change in Irish policy must, of course, be viewed in context. Britain was itself becoming highly protectionist, world trade was falling and real incomes throughout the western world were to suffer a disastrous decline. In an oft-quoted passage, Keynes himself lent his considerable authority to protectionist policies stating that: 'If I were an Irishman, I should find much to attract me in the economic outlook of your Government towards self-sufficiency'.[4] In addition to all this, relations were further exasperated by a dispute over land annuities which rapidly escalated into a damaging 'Economic War'.

The imposition of tariffs and quotas on British imports raised no particular legal difficulties. No formal trading agreement existed between the Irish Free State and the UK during the decade after 1922. Few tariffs existed on the Irish side and practically none on the British. Irish tariffs afforded imperial preference rates to imports of British origin. What happened after 1932 was a discrete and extensive increase in the level and range of protection. The average nominal tariff rose from 9 per cent in 1931 to 35 per cent in 1938 and quotas were applied to supplement this position where necessary.[5] The import share of domestic expenditure during the short period 1931–35 fell from 86 to 40 per cent in the case of footwear, from 88 to 40 per cent on linen piece goods, from 100 to 32 per cent on glass bottles.[6] Replacement of imports, mainly of British origin, by domestically-produced substitutes took place mostly in the case of consumer goods but some intermediate and capital goods imports were also affected.

Given the underdeveloped nature of Ireland's industrial base it was not surprising to find a quick response to the incentives for domestic production provided by these import restrictions. Government policy, however, was also directed to ensuring that, as far as possible, the domestic production should be undertaken and controlled by Irish nationals. Even the comparatively mild protection of the 1920s had encouraged British investors to take over manufacturing plants which would serve the Irish market. Dr Mary Daly, for example, finds that (foreigner and outsider can largely be equated with British):

foreign investment in Irish industry, mainly through the takeover of existing firms, increased during the 1920s as a result of the imposition of selective tariffs. By 1928 the tobacco industry was deemed to be largely under foreign control . . . Soap manufactures had virtually passed into the hands of the giant Lever Bros . . . while 50 per cent of confectionery output was in the hands of outsiders such as Crosse and Blackwell, Clarnico Murray, Rowntree and Macintosh.[7]

To prevent an intensification of this 'tariff-jumping' the Control of Manufactures Acts 1932 and 1934 stipulated that all new manufacturing establishments set up after 1 June 1932 which were not majority-Irish-owned would have to obtain a licence. However, the provisions of the Acts were widely circumvented. Many protected sectors were dominated by foreign concerns and by the late 1930s it was increasingly difficult to distinguish domestic and foreign companies. More fundamentally it became clear as the thirties progressed that the twin government policies of maximum industrial growth and maximum native ownership were in conflict. The conflict was in practice resolved by giving priority to industrial growth.

The main thrust of agricultural protectionism was directed against cereal, fruit and vegetable and sugar imports which would not have originated in – though they were often consigned through – Britain and Northern Ireland. The instruments used to control food imports were the same as for industrial goods. In addition, a guaranteed price was offered to domestic producers of wheat and export subsidies were given for butter, bacon and other goods. The effects were no less visible than in the case of manufactures. Wheat output rose twelve-fold between 1931 and 1938 and sugar beet 4.5 times.[8]

Superimposed on these dramatic changes in policy was the

Economic War. The dispute related to land annuities paid by Irish farmers on land acquired prior to Independence. Following the De Valera Government's refusal to transfer the annuities to London, the British government imposed penal taxes on Irish cattle exports. In the worst year of the War, 1934, these duties lay within the range 68–88 per cent of the value of the animal depending on age.[9] Dublin retaliated with duties on coal, cement, electrical goods, iron and steel manufactures, sugar and other goods. The most visible effects were felt by the Irish farmer. Cattle export prices, already suffering from the depressed world market conditions, plummeted to half their 1931 values in 1935. From 1935 things began to improve as a result of a succession of coal – cattle pacts which exchanged British coal for Irish cattle on a pound for pound basis and brought about a reduction in duties. The dispute was settled by the 1938 Anglo-Irish Agreement on terms which were generally regarded as favourable to Ireland. A lump sum of £10m was accepted as a final payment for land annuities (against an initial British demand of £100m representing their capital value). The British market was opened to Irish food and cattle exports and imperial preference was restored. In return Ireland undertook to afford preferential treatment to British goods and to review its existing import restrictions.

A further improvement in trading conditions was secured after the Second World War by the trade agreement of 1948 which linked the prices paid for Irish cattle and sheep to the prices received by British farmers. The quantity, and in some cases the prices, of other agricultural goods which would be accepted by Britain was also agreed. There was provision for a review of quotas on Irish agricultural exports to Britain and on British industrial exports to Ireland. Reflecting the changed circumstances of the time, the British undertook to maintain supplies of coal and the Irish government promised to economise on the use of hard currencies and to obtain the maximum amount of Marshall Aid, negotiated with the United States government, in order to relieve the strain on the dollar pool of the sterling area.[10]

The effects of worldwide protectionism on industrial and agricultural products, the Economic War and the Second World War were highly adverse to Irish foreign trade and living standards. Real incomes per head were no higher at the end of the 1930s than at the start of the decade. National income thereafter grew very slowly – by only 14 per cent between 1938 and 1947 compared with 84 per cent in Northern Ireland and 47 per cent in the UK as a whole.[11] True, an industrial base had been established and the Control of Manufactures Acts, despite their many loopholes, had ensured that a significant proportion of it was Irish controlled. But, as time would reveal, the foundations were unstable and incapable of supporting efficient growth.

The change in policy and in circumstance did not please all sections of the Irish economy. The imposition of British tariffs had induced some Irish firms to set up plants in England (prompted by the same motivation as British firms establishing subsidiaries in Ireland). Exports of beer, having fallen between 1932 and 1936, collapsed from 1.3 million barrels in 1936 to 294,000 barrels two years later when Guinness opened a brewery in Park Royal to avoid British export duties.[12] The rundown of the Ford plant in Cork and of the Jacobs biscuit factory in Dublin were prompted by much the same pressures. The consequences for agriculture were particularly severe. Net agricultural income declined in current value from £51m in 1929–30 to £32m in 1934–35 from which it recovered to only £43m in 1938–39.[13] These losses were much greater proportionately than were incurred by British and Northern Ireland farmers.

Perhaps the most enduring lesson concerned the continued dependence of Irish exports on the British market. Apart from the exceptional period of the Second World War, the prospect of which incidentally had softened British attitudes sufficiently to bring about the 1938 accord, Irish agricultural prosperity was closely tied to access to the British market and British agricultural policy. Even at the height of the Economic War, Ireland sold 91 per cent of her exports to the UK. The same proportion prevailed into the late 1940s and early 1950s. Attempts were made to find new markets on the Continent during the 1930s but without notable success.[14] The attempt to secure agricultural prosperity on the basis of self-sufficiency foundered because the domestic market was simply too small. Neither could export market diversification be achieved through the protected domestic industries. As later studies were to show, the very process of protection created a strong bias against exports.[15] Price and profit signals pointed to deeper penetration of the small domestic market rather than to the discovery of new markets in Britain and continental Europe.

TRADE LIBERALISATION AND EUROPEAN INTEGRATION

In a remarkable article written in 1959, Patrick Lynch, perhaps one of the most influential academic economists in the country at the time, propounded a view which must have sounded highly heretical to many of his contemporaries:

> to maintain the present standard of living and to strive to increase it, the inter-dependence of the Irish and British economies must be consciously recognised. Indeed if Irish economic development is to be planned intelligently in the context of the economic changes which the Common Market and the proposed Free Trade Area imply in Europe, a beginning should be made by explicitly establishing closer economic association with Britain.[16]

He attacked the Sinn Féin myth which identified political independence with economic self-sufficiency and which 'had been a decisive influence on public thinking and policy for more than two generations'. He had some novel views on emigration, arguing that Irish migration to Britain was regional rather than international in character and that emigrants had not only improved their own living standards by leaving the country but had also made it possible 'to afford a standard of living that could not be maintained if Irish political independence implied the obligation to cater on their own terms for all the people born in Ireland since the state was established'.

But why closer association with Britain? By reducing tariffs and/or increasing the degree of preference on imports, Ireland could offer something useful to the British government. The Irish market was then and has continued to be one of the principal outlets in Europe for British exporters. Hence Ireland had something of value to offer the British government as a bargaining counter in exchange for concessions which Westminster might be prepared to offer to Irish exports.

The main *quid pro quo* from Ireland's perspective was improved access for agricultural produce on the British market. The point was made that since Ireland had a comparative advantage in agriculture both Britain and Ireland could benefit from an increase in such trade. On the industrial side the gains were more speculative – British tariffs on Irish manufactured imports were very low – and Lynch was not very forthcoming on this topic. An interesting reflection of how times and opinions had changed was his view that 'Irish tax incentives to export industries should induce British firms to establish plants here', preferably aided by improved access to the UK market. The argument for freer trade had of course been strongly canvassed earlier in the White Papers, *Economic Development* (1958) and *The First Programme for Economic Expansion* (1958) on the grounds that Ireland could not remain isolated from European moves toward trade liberalisation and that, with suitable adaptation, Irish industrial efficiency could be increased sufficiently to meet the challenge of foreign competition. The dichotomy between the agricultural sector and the industrial sector was less pronounced then than it is now. Much of Ireland's industrial expansion was foreseen as emerging from agricultural-based industries, notably beef and dairy processing.

The period from the mid-1950s saw a steady progression towards what economists call 'outward-looking policies'. The Export Profits Tax Relief Scheme was introduced and the Control of Manufactures Acts repealed in the 1950s. A trade agreement was concluded with Britain in 1960 which formalised the price-link for store cattle and reaffirmed previous arrangements. Attention was, of course, then being focused on the possible terms and consequences of Irish and UK membership of the European Community. With the collapse of the EEC negotiations in 1963, the way was clear to conclusion of the Anglo-Irish Free Trade Area Agreement (AIFTA) between Ireland and the UK which was signed in December 1965 and came into effect in 1966.

Under the terms of AIFTA, the Irish government undertook to eliminate most protective duties on non-agricultural imports from the UK, by ten annual tariff reductions of 10 per cent each. Average nominal tariffs on UK imports, prior to the agreement, were estimated as 20 per cent for consumer goods, 14 per cent for capital goods and 9 per cent for intermediate goods. Quantitative import restrictions and the 'protective' element in certain revenue duties were also to be eliminated. Separate arrangements were made for agricultural and processed foodstuffs and for certain sensitive products such as motor vehicles.[17]

In return the British government removed tariffs on Irish manufactures. This concession was relevant mainly to certain sections of the textile, clothing and footwear industries; only about £5m of Irish manufactured exports were dutiable, about 15 per cent of total manufactured exports from Ireland in Britain. The main impact applied to the agriculture sector where the British fatstock guarantee was extended to a higher tonnage of Irish exports, subsidies were available at an earlier period to store cattle, the butter quota was almost doubled and concessions made to exports of cheddar cheese.

A cost-benefit survey of the Agreement showed that, at the half-way stage, the increase in Irish exports to Britain just about equalled the increase in Irish imports from Britain.[18] This suggests a broadly favourable impact on welfare provided it is remembered that it is the value of the exchange and not the accumulation of trade surpluses and deficits which determines gain from trade. British investment in Ireland increased during the period – and by 1973, over 29,000 people were employed in British manufacturing subsidiaries – but it is doubtful if much of this increase was specifically related to the Anglo-Irish Free Trade Area. Competition in agricultural export markets was fierce and Irish food exports had to be heavily subsidised by the government. Nevertheless, a strategic objective of the Agreement was to show that Ireland was committed to a policy of trade liberalisation, that Irish industry was prepared to take on foreign competition and that Ireland therefore had all the qualifications needed for accession to the European Economic Community when the opportunity of re-opening negotiations on that issue would arise. On this broader interpretation of its aims, the Agreement was successful from an Irish perspective. The Republic became a member of the European Economic Community in 1973.

Outward-looking policies and membership of the Community brought with them an unexpected prize – diminished economic dependence on Britain. The inward-looking policies of the post-1932 period had as one of their objectives the diminution of dependence on Britain and in this they had singularly failed. The advocates of liberalisation had taken it for granted that their policies would be based on closer integration with Britain. They argued that, to the extent that Ireland became better-off as a result, its political independence would be enhanced. Economic dependence and political integrity were not antithetical. Yet, as the 1960s wore on, it became increasingly apparent that the geographical concentration of Irish trade was changing rapidly. Between 1960 and 1984, the proportion of Irish exports sold to the UK fell from 74 per cent to 34 per cent. The share of British goods in Ireland's manufactured imports also declined sharply. The cause of the fall in export dependence on the UK can be traced, in the case of manufactures, to the upsurge in foreign direct investment by the United States and continental European firms which set up subsidiaries in Ireland in response to fiscal incentives, lower costs and the promise of access to the European market. For these firms, the European market was the target. Established British firms and Irish firms continued to rely predominantly on the British market. In the case of agricultural goods, the opening of the continental European market, from which Irish produce had been virtually excluded since 1964, was the main force for change. Under the new regime, there was the added bonus that the terms of access to the British market were decided in Brussels rather than being solely at the discretion of Westminster.

The decline in the UK share of Irish imports happened despite rather than because of the new trade arrangements. The UK share of most manufactured categories fell from the 1950s onwards in the Irish market as well as elsewhere in the world because of the lack of competitiveness of British goods relative to other industrial countries. But because its initial share of Irish industrial imports was high and Irish industrial imports were growing very rapidly relative to non-industrial imports, the UK's share of total Irish imports stayed at around 50 per cent for about twenty years. Recently, however, it has started to decline.

EMS AND THE STERLING LINK

For many years, British and Irish notes and currency had circulated throughout Ireland freely and interchangeably. After 1979 all that changed. As Brendan Walsh put it: 'Membership of the European Monetary System (EMS) had a more dramatic and tangible impact on Ireland than membership of the EEC itself. This is because within weeks after the formation of the system our currency departed from the one-to-one no-margins parity that had been maintained with sterling since 1829'.[19] The break in parity between the Irish pound and sterling had been considered a number of times since 1922. Immediately after Independence, fears were expressed about the deflationary effects of an overvalued pound on the Irish economy following sterling's return to the gold standard. (A separate Irish pound was not established until 1928.) Later, in 1931 when Britain left the gold standard, a collapse of sterling was feared. The Minister for Finance at that time, Ernest Blythe, made it clear that should such a collapse occur, Ireland would have to break the sterling parity. Again, in 1949, there was debate over the wisdom of letting the Irish pound devalue in line with the British pound. In each case, however, the balance of least disadvantage was judged to rest with maintenance of the status quo. In the 1970s, the inflationary consequences of the sterling parity caused concern and the possibility of breaking the link was again considered. However, it was not until 1978, with the formation of the EMS, that the opportunity of moving to a different exchange rate regime really became practicable.

At the time, the EMS promised to provide two advantages of overwhelming importance: (a) a stronger and less inflationary currency regime; and (b) exchange rate stability with currencies accounting for 75 per cent of Irish trade. The last advantage, predicated on participation of the UK in the system, had the added attraction of conforming to the effective exchange rate target which the Central Bank was considering as an alternative to the sterling link prior to EMS.

In the event, the UK decided against participating in the EMS. The Governor of the Central Bank explained the choice facing Ireland in the following terms:

> an EMS which included the UK was attractive – though not necessarily painless. The real problem emerged when it became clear that the UK might not join. To put it bluntly, the issue turned on whether, granted that it would be right to join if the UK did, would it be right not to join if the UK didn't? The decision to join without the UK, was not an easy one. Factors which weighed in the balance included the alternatives open to us, the inappropriateness of an indefinite prolongation of the sterling link, the benefits in terms of a reduction in inflation to be obtained from adherence to a hard currency regime, a commitment to a major Community initiative, the extent to which the new system differed from the old and, of course, Community support in the form of resource transfers.[20]

The new exchange rate arrangements promised exchange rate stability covering only 30 per cent of Irish trade instead of the 75 per cent coverage which would have materialised had the UK joined.

The one-to-one parity with sterling was broken in March 1979. The sterling/Irish pound rate has fluctuated considerably since then. The last quarter of 1980 saw a significant rise in sterling. From IR £1 = 0.88p sterling in September 1980 the sterling/pound exchange rate fell to IR £1 = 0.74p sterling by mid-February 1981. It averaged 88p in the first quarter of 1983, before falling to 78p in the fourth quarter. More recently, the Irish pound has risen from 75p sterling in August 1985 to 95p sterling in March 1986 only to fall again to 87p a few weeks later. Thus, membership of the EMS has been associated with large periodic swings in the bilateral exchange rate with sterling (and the dollar) and, at least until 1985, with a declining nominal effective exchange rate. The history of sterling/IR£ exchange fluctuations since 1979 bears out only too well the worries implicit in Dr Murray's admission that the decision to join the EMS without the UK was not an easy one.

The problem is that the Irish monetary authorities are, in a sense, riding two horses: on the one hand, EMS obligations must be adhered to which means infrequent re-alignments and then only after consultation with EMS partners; on the other hand, there is concern that the Irish pound/sterling rate should be consistent with other policy objectives. If sterling strengthens, the Irish authorities must seek a revaluation or else accept the consequences of higher inflation. During the initial period of the EMS, sterling did strengthen; the Irish economy 'imported' inflation from Britain and inevitably, the promise of low inflation had to be disappointed. If sterling weakens – and it has done most recently between August 1985 and March 1986 – the authorities can either do nothing in the expectation that the loss in competitiveness will be transitory or else seek a depreciation. A small depreciation within the EMS was obtained in March 1983. Even more dramatic was the 8 per cent depreciation in the IR£ in August 1986 which was a direct response to the fall in sterling and underlined the difficulty of making 'stability within the EMS' the sole objective of exchange rate policy.

The break with sterling, therefore, has had a highly visible impact. This impact has been felt not only through the break in parity but also in the application for the first time of exchange control regulations between the two islands (and between Northern Ireland and the Republic). Looking to the future, it is clear that Irish interests would strongly support participation by the UK in the EMS currency arrangements. In the matter of exchange controls, the present Governor of the Central Bank of Ireland, Tomas Ó Cofaigh, while defending the controls as having served a constructive purpose in the formative years of the EMS 'when there was considerable uncertainty as to how the Irish pound would perform', has stated that 'our system of exchange control must be kept under review, with a view to liberalisation where this is possible and prudent'.[21]

The break with sterling occurred as an incidental and unwanted consequence of the decision to join the EMS. The diminished dependence on the UK in trade and investment enabled Ireland to survive successfully, if not altogether comfortably, within the System. As in the case of trade policy, although over a much shorter time span, there is a sense in which the wheel has come full circle. Having broken the link in 1979, the desire now is to see it restored, although not necessarily at parity. Restoration of the link by full British EMS participation would then open the way to liberalisation of exchange controls and a return to the *status quo ante*.

ANGLO-IRISH INTERDEPENDENCE SINCE 1979

Ireland's dependence on the UK economy has declined during the past two decades. Trade has become more diversified geographically, American and European subsidiaries dominate the one-third of Irish industry which is foreign-controlled, agricultural trade is governed by the Common Agricultural Policy and the sterling link has been broken. Irish people are probably more conscious of the extent of decoupling of the two economies than of the ties which still remain. Nevertheless a recent study of the effects of post-1979 structural change in the UK shows just how close the ties still are.[22]

Structural change since 1979 has affected all sectors of the British economy. From being a large net importer of oil,

Britain became a major world oil producer and net exporter. Manufacturing output fell by 17 per cent between early 1979 and late 1980 and has recovered at a slow pace since then. Numbers unemployed exceeded three million, the highest figure for any time in the last forty-five years. The composition of exports and imports changed dramatically. In 1983, for the first time since the Industrial Revolution the UK became a net importer of manufactured goods in peace-time. The decline in its share of world trade in manufacturing goods accelerated. At the same time inflation fell steeply and, buoyed up by North Sea oil and high interest rates, sterling became a stronger currency. Policy changes relating to trade unions, taxation, privatisation, deregulation and public sector finances altered the business environment in a fundamental way.

These events have had important implications for Ireland. First, the decline in Britain's manufacturing output has been responsible for large job losses in British manufacturing subsidiaries operating in Ireland. By end-1985 40 per cent of the jobs in British subsidiaries existing in 1979 had disappeared and the process of attrition is continuing. In absolute terms this involved a decline in employment in these subsidiaries from 24,000 in 1979 (one-third of employment in foreign-owned plants in Ireland), to 14,000 in 1985 (less than one-fifth of employment in foreign-owned plants). As already mentioned, the UK share of foreign investment in Ireland had been declining steeply since the 1960s – it accounted for 50 per cent of total employment in overseas plants even as late as 1973 – but the pace of decline has accelerated since 1979. Since UK subsidiaries have tended to concentrate exports on the British market, the decline in their activities in Ireland has been associated with a further reduction in the proportion of Irish manufactured exports finding a market in Britain. Significantly, most of the British firms closing down had been set up under the protectionist era.

Second, the rise in unemployment in Britain has exacerbated the unemployment problem in Ireland. There is a close statistical relationship between unemployment rates in the two countries. As labour market conditions in Britain deteriorate, Irish workers who might otherwise have emigrated are slower to do so. Also Irish people in Britain look homeward for job opportunities. This puts upward pressures on the unemployment rate in Ireland.

Third, while the high value of sterling, and the accompanying decline in the value of the Irish pound, gave Irish exporters a competitive advantage during the period 1979–81, the business environment in Britain has improved considerably in recent years. Particularly in the area of taxation, the advantage has swung away from Ireland which ever since independence had tended, as a matter of policy, to offer a more favourable tax climate.[23]

Surprisingly in view of the trade links between the two countries, Irish exports did not suffer as a result of the recession. This had nothing to do with preferential treatment or with the type of goods exported from Ireland. Rather it can be explained by the nature of the British recession which was accompanied by an upsurge rather than, as is normally the case, a decline in import demand.

Recent experience therefore reinforces the conclusion that, while Anglo-Irish interdependence has weakened, it is far from broken.

FROM EXCESSIVE INTIMACY TO A WIDER EMBRACE

For fifty years after Independence, Anglo-Irish trade and investment problems were dealt with almost entirely on a bilateral basis. Throughout the period Britain was clearly the more powerful country. Its ability to inflict damage on the Irish economy was totally disproportionate to any retaliatory measures which the Irish government could devise. Even during the Second World War, when Irish food was in greater demand, the balance of advantage was by no means all one way. The dependence of the Irish economy on raw materials and intermediate goods transhipped via British ports was no less acute than Britain's need of Irish agricultural produce.

Britain's response to this position of economic strength

was, it must be said, a great deal more enlightened than the past history of the two nations would have led one to expect. There was no dogmatic insistence on absolute reciprocity in matters relating to access in Britain for Irish goods, capital or people and, in the resolution of the Economic War in 1938, there was evidence of generosity on the British side. This happy conclusion was greatly assisted by the professional understanding between Treasury and Department of Finance officials, so convincingly documented by Fanning,[24] and by the personal intervention of distinguished British civil servants. Fanning cites Warren Fisher, Permanent Secretary to the Treasury, who minuted prior to the resolution of the annuities dispute:

> I feel strongly that it would pay England in the long run and in every way to take a generous view of this most unhappy financial tangle.[25]

Enlightened self-interest played an unusually dominant role in this aspect of Anglo-Irish relations.

Membership of the Community has changed the focus of the two countries' relationships. It has put an end to the era of bilateral trade agreements, trade-offs, threats and retaliation. Since 1973 Ireland has moved from being a minor entity, dominated economically by Britain, to membership of a Community of highly developed economies in which it has equal rights and obligations. Within the Community, of course, some nations are more equal than others! The differences between Britain and Ireland on the subject of agricultural prices are now fought out in Brussels rather than in London and Dublin. Cross border trade and cooperation between Northern Ireland and the Republic has also received encouragement at European level. Anglo-Irish economic discussions centre increasingly on matters of European concern such as EEC regional policy and the Community budget. The assessment of Eamonn Gallagher of the EEC Commission serves as a succinct summary of how relations have changed:

> the effects of common United Kingdom and Irish membership of the Community and particularly their attitudes to the emerging Community are so great that Anglo-Irish relations can hardly now be usefully discussed except in that context. This . . . is healthy for both

partners as it substitutes a greatly wider embrace for what has been an excessive intimacy.[26]

Acknowledgement: The author is grateful to Elaine Byrne, P. J. Drudy and Professor P. Lynch for helpful comments.

REFERENCES

1. Dermot McAleese, 'The foreign sector', in N. J. Gibson and J. E. Spencer (eds), *Economic Activity in Ireland* (Dublin, 1977). See also Appendix table at end of chapter.
2. Quotation from F. List, *National System of Political Economy*, cited in Richard Davis, *Arthur Griffith and Non Violent Sinn Féin*, (Dublin, 1974).
3. The concern of the Provisional and the Free State governments with financial stability, the necessity for such concern given the dubiety with which Irish bankers initially reacted to government requests for loans and funding and the constraining impact of this concern on economic policy are described in Ronan Fanning, 'The impact of Independence', in F. S. L. Lyons (ed.), *Bicentenary Essays: Bank of Ireland 1783–1983* (Dublin, 1983).
4. J. M. Keynes, 'Economics self-sufficiency', *Studies*, 1933, p. 177, cited in J. Meenan, *The Irish Economy since 1922* (Liverpool, 1972), p. 320.
5. W. J. L. Ryan, 'Measurements of tariff levels in Ireland', *Journal of the Statistical and Social Inquiry Society of Ireland*, 1948–49. For an excellent survey of Irish trade policy since the 1930s, see chapter 3, 'From protection to free trade – the Irish experience', in T. K. Whitaker, *Interests*, (Dublin, 1983).
6. F. Flynn, 'The development of home industry', *Administration*, Vol. 20, No. 1, 1972.
7. Mary Daly, 'An Irish Ireland for business?: the Control of Manufactures Acts, 1922 and 1934', *Irish Historical Studies*, Vol. 24, 1984, p. 248.
8. See John A. Murphy, *Ireland in the Twentieth Century* (Dublin, 1975), chapter 4 for a succinct analysis of the period 1932–39.
9. David Johnson, *The Interwar Economy in Ireland: Studies in Irish Economic and Social History* (Dublin 1985).
10. James Meenan, *The Irish Economy since 1922* (Liverpool, 1970), p. 79.
11. Johnson, *Interwar Economy*, p. 43.
12. John W. O'Hagan and Kyran McStay, *The Evolution of Manufacturing Industry in Ireland*, Confederation of Irish industry, (Dublin, 1981), pp. 15–16.

13. R. O'Connor and C. Guiomard, 'Agricultural output in the Irish Free State Area before and after Independence', *Irish Economic and Social History*, Vol. 12, 1985, Table 1.
14. Meenan (*The Irish Economy*, p. 99) notes that bilateral agreements were entered into with Spain (exchange of Irish eggs for oranges), Belgium (outlets for Irish exports of cattle and butter) and Germany but these arrangements did not open new channels of any importance.
15. Dermot McAleese, *Effective Tariffs and the Structure of Industrial Protection in Ireland*, ESRI Paper no 62, (Dublin, 1971).
16. Patrick Lynch, 'The economics of Independence: some unsettled questions of Irish economics', *Administration*, Vol. 7, No 2, 1959. Reprinted in B. Chubb and P. Lynch (eds), *Economic Development and Planning* (Dublin, 1969), p. 132.
17. Dermot McAleese and John Martin, *Irish Manufactured Imports from the UK in the Sixties: The Effects of AIFTA*, ESRI Paper No 79 (Dublin, 1973).
18. McAleese and Martin, *Irish Manufactured Imports*.
19. Brendan Walsh, 'Ireland's membership of the European Monetary System: expectations, out-turn and prospects', in P. J. Drudy and Dermot McAleese (eds), *Ireland and the European Community, Irish Studies Vol. 3* (Cambridge, 1984), p. 173.
20. Quotation from Dr C. Murray and text drawn from Dermot McAleese, 'Political independence, economic growth and the role of economic policy', in P. J. Drudy (ed.), *Ireland: Land, Politics and People, Irish Studies Vol. 2* (Cambridge, 1982), pp. 281–4.
21. Tomas Ó Cofaigh, 'The development of financial markets in Ireland', *Central Bank of Ireland Quarterly Bulletin*, Autumn 1985, p. 81.
22. Dermot McAleese, 'Anglo-Irish interdependence: effects of post-1979 changes in the British economy on Ireland', *Irish Banking Review*, Spring, 1986.
23. T. K. Daniel, 'Griffith on his noble head: the determinants of Cumann na nGaedheal economic policy 1922–32', *Irish Economic and Social History*, Vol. 3, 1976, p. 59.
24. Ronan Fanning, *The Irish Department of Finance 1922–58* (Dublin, 1978).
25. Fanning, *Irish Department of Finance*, p. 297.
26. Eamonn Gallagher, 'Anglo-Irish relations in the European community', *Irish Studies in International Affairs*, Vol. 2, No 1, 1985, p. 35.

6 · Migration between Ireland and Britain since Independence

P. J. DRUDY

The relationship between Ireland and Britain has been influenced in no small measure by the movement of population. The flow has of course been in both directions but the number of Irish settling in Britain has far exceeded the number of British in Ireland. For centuries, large-scale temporary movement of Irish migratory workers had taken place. By the end of the eighteenth century migration to Britain on a permanent basis had also been established on a substantial scale. Thus, by 1841 the British Census of Population recorded a total of 419,000 Irish-born living in Britain; within two further decades this figure had almost doubled, reflecting the flight from appalling poverty and hunger in Ireland during and after the Great Famine of 1845–49. Movement to Britain dropped off towards the end of the century when post-famine emigrants flocked in massive numbers to the United States. During the period 1841–60 some 1.7 million Irish had disembarked at American ports. By the time Ireland achieved independence in 1922 a further 2.4 million people had left for the New World. Whatever the destination was, we can be fairly confident that at least eight million persons emigrated from Ireland between 1801 and 1921 – a number equal to the entire Irish population at its peak, just before the Great Famine.[1]

As a result of emigration the population of Ireland showed consistent decline. This was in marked contrast to the situation prevailing in most European countries during this period. In 1841, the population of Ireland – north and south – was eight million. By the end of the century the population had almost halved and the decline continued up to independence in 1922 – the most significant losses occurring in the twenty-six counties which comprise the present Republic.

Many felt that the problem of emigration, as well as other difficulties, would be alleviated if only Ireland could break the link with Britain. Whatever the arguments for independence, it did not put an end to Irish emigration which continued on a substantial scale for the first forty years of the new state. During most of the period however Britain, and not the United States, became the destination for the vast majority of emigrants. It was not until the 1960s that a marked transformation in Irish demographic patterns became obvious and the Republic commenced on a phase of significant population growth – so significant indeed that, in stark contrast to previous periods, the country had the fastest growth rate in western Europe. Furthermore, substantial 'return migration' to Ireland was to occur throughout much of the 1970s. In the late 1970s however net emigration resumed once more. This chapter first examines the extent and causes of emigration since the 1920s. It then assesses the nature of population growth and reduced emigration from the 1960s. Lastly, it looks at the re-emergence of substantial emigration in recent years and assesses its causes and implications.

Table 6.1 sets out details of the natural increase (births minus deaths), net emigration and population change for the Republic of Ireland since 1926. The birth rate has been consistently higher than the death rate so that a positive natural increase has always been recorded. However, net emigration was so high in the years up to 1961 that the natural increase was depleted and the total population was reduced. Net emigration accelerated from 16,700 per annum in the 1926–36 period to 42,400 per annum in 1956–61. With a relatively small population base, such losses, especially on the scale experienced in the 1950s could be viewed just as seriously as much of the mass emigration in the pre-1900 era. During the three and a half decades between 1926 and 1961 the total net emigration was 882,000 and the population declined by 154,000 persons. Consistent losses were recorded in practically every county in the Republic so that by 1961 only four counties contained larger populations than they had held in 1926. The most notable of these was Dublin county which,

Table 6.1. *Average annual natural increase, net emigration and population change, 1926–86*

Period	Average annual natural increase			Average annual net emigration			Average annual population change		
	Males	Females	Total	Males	Females	Total	Males	Females	Total
1926–36	8,612	7,706	16,318	−7,255	−9,420	−16,675	+1,357	−1,734	−357
1936–46	8,700	8,680	17,380	−11,258	−7,454	−18,712	−2,558	+1,226	−1,332
1946–51	12,699	12,804	25,503	−10,309	−14,075	−24,384	+2,390	−1,271	+1,119
1951–56	12,923	13,964	26,887	−21,657	−17,696	−39,353	−8,734	−3,732	−12,466
1956–61	12,639	13,777	26,416	−21,914	−20,486	−42,400	−9,276	−6,709	−15,985
1961–66	14,019	15,234	29,253	−7,523	−8,598	−16,121	+6,496	+6,636	+13,132
1966–71	14,295	15,335	29,630	−4,950	−5,831	−10,781	+9,345	+9,504	+18,849
1971–79	17,030	18,099	35,129	+7,659	+5,958	+13,617	+24,689	+24,057	+48,746
1979–81	19,647	20,470	40,117	−1,606	−917	−2,523	+18,041	+19,553	+37,594
1981–86	16,345	17,474	33,820	−8,717	−6,345	−15,062	+7,629	+11,129	+18,758

Source: Census of Population of Ireland, Vol. 1, 1981 and Central Statistics Office, Dublin.

together with the County Borough, increased from 505,600 to 718,300 during this period. The counties of Kildare, Louth and Meath, also in the east of the country, increased too, but at a more modest rate. All other counties registered fairly persistent decline, with those in the west and north west faring worst of all. The most severely affected areas were also the least urbanised and those most heavily dependent on the agricultural industry. Thus, Leitrim declined by 40 per cent during the three and a half decades in question; Cavan by 31 per cent; Roscommon and Mayo by 29 per cent; and Monaghan by 28 per cent. Population loss and emigration during this period were thus largely rural-based, consisting predominantly of those leaving agriculture or the non-agricultural population from small towns and villages throughout rural Ireland. In addition to this, the exodus consisted predominantly of the young and most active – between 1946 and 1961 some 75 per cent of the net loss was in the age group below 34 years of age. Can we identify the main factors accounting for this exodus?

The newly-independent state, established in 1922, inherited an economic structure which was largely under-developed under the British influence. In order to protect British commercial interests, Irish industry had been suppressed during the seventeenth and eighteenth centuries. During the nineteenth and early twentieth centuries, when a pattern of free trade was imposed, Ireland was likewise unable to compete on equal terms with Britain in most areas of industrial activity and it was only in the north east of the country that any significant industrial development took place.[2] Ireland thus remained heavily dependent on the agricultural industry throughout this extended period and at Independence, despite a significant change in the pattern of land ownership, the structure of agriculture left much to be desired. This inheritance was not an unimportant determinant of the slow patterns of development and emigration, at least in the early decades after independence. Although Ireland achieved political independence in 1922, her economic dependence was by no means at an end – Britain was to remain a crucial destination for Irish exports and for migrant labour.[3]

In addition to this, there was no substantial period in the decades after Independence, even up to the 1950s, which could be regarded as 'normal' in any meaningful sense. Civil war was followed closely by a world recession, the widespread erection of trade barriers, the 'Economic War' with Britain on which Ireland depended for an export market, and the Second World War in which Ireland chose to remain neutral. These various events influenced, and perhaps forced, successive Irish governments towards policies which, however well-intentioned, had not all the desired domestic effects. Thus, in order to build up native Irish industry, strong protectionist policies were pursued, especially from the 1930s, and the emphasis on the erection of tariff barriers lasted, with the exception of the Second World War period, right up to the 1960s.[4] These policies proved effective in developing new industries and expanding older ones and they secured substantial growth in industrial output during particular periods. However, they did not result in the desired self-sufficiency. A strong import propensity, accompanied by poor export performance, therefore resulted in recurrent balance of payments difficulties in the late 1940s and 1950s. In addition to this, the growth of industrial output during this period did not result in the level of job creation required to absorb the large numbers leaving agriculture in the post-Independence decades.

At Independence Ireland was a predominantly small-farm economy with two-thirds of the agricultural holdings having less than thirty acres. This situation was accompanied, particularly in the western areas of the country, by certain physical difficulties such as fragmentation of holdings and high proportions of poor land. In such 'marginal' areas a pattern of late inheritance, an unbalanced demographic structure and slow progress in improving the structure of land holdings resulted in retarded agricultural development, low relative incomes and poor employment prospects. In more prosperous agricultural areas in the south and south east of the country the structure of agriculture was rather better but in such areas increased mechanisation reduced the demand for labour. This reduction in 'labour requirements' meant that there was little incentive for young people to remain on farms in any part of Ireland.[5] The exodus from agriculture was not of course confined to Ireland; it was occurring in all European countries. Such a trend need not be regarded as undesirable if those leaving agriculture can be absorbed into non-agricultural employment. However, for the majority in Ireland this was not to be.

During the period 1926–61 the number of people employed in agriculture declined by over 272,300. During the same period only 101,800 non-agricultural jobs (provided either by the state or private enterprise) became available. The net loss of jobs was thus 170,500 and about half this loss was accounted for by areas in the west and north west – Galway, Mayo, Sligo, Leitrim and Donegal. This absence of sufficient opportunities to earn a livelihood especially in rural Ireland was a crucial factor in influencing people to emigrate – as mentioned above, it was the 'rural' counties which bore the brunt of the population loss.

The foregoing discussion has emphasised a variety of 'push' factors which influenced migration from Ireland. There was, in addition, the 'pull' of better employment opportunities outside Ireland, particularly in Britain and the United States. Furthermore, these two destinations often offered better social amenities, freedom from control of family and small community life in Ireland, and for some, an escape from the perceived constraints of Irish Catholicism and Ulster Protestantism.[6] They also presented the Irish with little or no difficulties of language or barriers of race.[7] Britain and the United States were thus major attractions for the Irish, both north and south.

During the period 1876–1921 the Commission on Emigration had estimated that 84 per cent of Irish emigrants went to the United States compared to only 8 per cent to Britain.[8] This situation was to change markedly in the years after Independence. Table 6.2 presents estimates of net emigration to various destinations and indicates that the United States accounted for 54 per cent of total net emigration

Table 6.2. *Estimates of net emigration from the Republic of Ireland, by main destination, 1926–61*

	'Overseas' to United States	Other[a] 'overseas'	Elsewhere (mainly Britain)	Total
1926–36[b]	90,416	9,429	66,906	166,751
1936–46[b]	—	—	187,111	187,111
1946–51[b]	15,875	3,506	100,187	119,568
1951–56[c]	13,975	7,956	174,832	196,763
1956–61[c]	26,842	12,854	172,307	212,003

Notes:
[a] 'Overseas' refers to areas outside Europe.
[b] Statistics prior to 1954 refer to travel by sea only. The 1926–36 figures are from 'emigration and immigration' statistics published in the *Irish Trade Journal*.
[c] In addition to sea travel, statistics from 1954 include those travelling by air to whom passports were issued for the purposes of entering permanent employment 'overseas'. They do not however account for those entering the Republic by air since complete details were not available – on the basis of other immigration statistics, this probably amounted to at least 1,000 per annum.
Source: Census of Population and *Irish Trade Journal* and *Statistical Bulletin*, various years.

during the period 1926–36. During subsequent decades net emigration to the United States fell dramatically and only revived to some extent during the peak period of exodus in the late 1950s. One can arrive at a similar conclusion by examining data giving the *gross* number of Irish immigrants entering the United States. For example, the gross figure during the 1926–31 decade was about 24,000 per annum; by 1956–61 during the heavy outflow from Ireland the figure had dropped to 7,300 per annum.[9] Britain thus became the most favoured destination. Further evidence of this is provided in Table 6.3 which shows a dramatic increase in the number of Irish-born residents in Britain, both from the Republic and Northern Ireland during the three decades from 1931 to 1961. During that period the number born in the Republic and resident in Britain rose by 359,000; that for Northern Ireland by 87,000.

Table 6.3. *Irish-born residents in Britain, 1931–81*

	Born in Irish Republic	Born in N. Ireland	Total
1931	367,424	137,961	505,385
1951	537,709	178,319	716,028
1961	726,121	224,857	950,978
1971	709,235	248,595	957,830
1981	607,428	242,969	850,397

Source: *Census of Population*, (Britain).

A variety of factors were responsible for the significant switch from the United States to Britain. An immigrant quota system was introduced for the first time in the United States in the Quota Act of 1921 in order to cope with the considerable inflow from Europe after the First World War. The Immigration Act of 1924 reduced the admissable annual quota further and immigrants were required to obtain visas from the American consul in the country of origin. In 1924 the quota for the present Republic of Ireland was 28,567 and in 1929 it was reduced to 17,853. During the depression years of the 1930s restrictions were also placed on persons without adequate funds or job prospects and 'guarantees' as to their solvency were also required. Consequently, the total inflow to the United States dropped dramatically, and most country quotas, including the Irish one, remained unfilled. This situation was to remain through the 1930s and until the end of the Second World War – during the decade 1936 to 1946 gross Irish emigration to the United States was a mere 5,000 persons. Although emigration to the United States did increase after the War and the quota system remained in being, the above pattern was to persist in later years. The quota system remained in operation until 1965 when it was abolished by the Immigration and Nationality Act. Until that time the Irish and indeed western hemisphere immigrants in general had received preferential treatment. Henceforth they were to find permanent entry to the United States much more difficult.[10]

In contrast to the increasing restrictions in America since the 1920s, Britain continued after Independence to offer complete freedom of entry to the Irish. Because of the War, restrictions on travel between Ireland and Britain were introduced in June 1940 and permission to travel would only be given in cases of 'national importance'. However, the serious need for labour in Britain for the war effort meant that the volume of migration between the two countries was not in fact seriously affected, although movement within Britain was restricted. It was the 'pull' of employment opportunities created by the Second World War which gave a renewed impetus to Irish emigration to Britain. The Irish catered for the requirements of the British economy during the War and post-war years when there was an acute shortage of labour in a number of key industries, not easily filled by native labour. The War also enabled the Irish to enter a wider range of occupations than the traditional areas of civil engineering, building and domestic service, and this occupational diversity was to continue in the post-war years. Freedom of access was also re-affirmed in the 1949 Ireland Act in which Britain recognised the Republic of Ireland. Freedom of access to both countries for British and Irish citizens was to remain in the years ahead.

In the Republic of Ireland the year 1961 marked the beginning of a phase of population growth and declining net emigration which seemed astonishing by comparison with previous trends. Thus, between 1961 and 1971 the total population increased by 160,000. Net emigration (all destinations) continued throughout the 1960s but at a reduced level – 16,100 per annum during 1961–66 and 11,700 per annum during 1966–71. Finally, between 1971 and 1979 a net inflow figure of 13,600 per annum was recorded (see Table 6.1) and the total population increased by some 390,000. It is important to point out that this net inflow of population during the 1970s was largely due to the scale of the gross inflows rather than to a dramatic decline in the size of gross outflows. As we shall see, gross outflows continued to be significant for certain groups during this and more recent periods. It should also be

Table 6.4. *Migration flows by country of birth, 1971–81 (000s)*

Age group	Country of birth				Total
	Irish Republic	N. Ireland	Britain	Other countries	
0–14	−12.1	+6.0	+43.5	+9.9	+47.3
15–24	−33.2	+3.7	+14.1	+5.2	−10.2
25–34	−15.0	+4.6	+5.9	+3.4	−1.1
35–44	+31.9	+2.6	+3.8	+1.3	+39.6
45–64	+6.1	+1.4	+1.3	+1.0	+9.8
65+	+16.8	+0.7	+0.6	+0.1	+18.2
Total all ages	−5.4	+19.0	+69.3	+21.0	+103.9

Source: Central Statistics Office, Dublin and Garvey (1985).

appreciated that, despite heavy outflows in the post-war periods, there has been a fairly consistent, if modest, inflow of population born outside Ireland. Thus, during the period 1946–61 there was a net gain of some 20,000 persons born outside the Republic of Ireland – the vast majority (13,800) from Britain; during the 1961–71 period, there was a net gain of some 51,000 – again the majority (36,500) from Britain.[11] The various flows for the 1971–81 period are set out in Table 6.4. This table shows a total net migration to Ireland of 104,000 persons during the decade. Garvey has estimated that 63,000 of these were married persons, most of whom had probably emigrated to Britain in the 1950s.[12] In addition, it will be noted that the inflow included substantial numbers of young children – almost 44,000 of these had been born in Britain. The brunt of the inflow thus came from Britain, but there was also a net inflow of 19,000 from Northern Ireland during this period, much of this due to the political difficulties there.

The dramatic change in the pattern of net migration can be attributed to a variety of 'push' and 'pull' factors. On this occasion, however, the net inflow to Ireland can be attributed largely to the 'pull' of improved economic circumstances in

Ireland. Although of lesser importance it also seems likely that reduced employment opportunities made Britain a less attractive option than it had been in the post-war era.[13] We concentrate here on the importance of the 'pull' of the improved economic environment in Ireland.

Even from the early 1950s governments in Ireland were beginning to recognise the difficulties of relying unduly on protectionist and self-sufficiency policies which characterised the post-independence decades. Whatever the advantages of such policies, they were not creating sufficient jobs to stem the tide of emigration. Thus, the Capital Investment Advisory Committee, appointed in 1955, strongly argued for a change of direction. The White Paper on *Economic Development* in 1958 and, arising from this, the *First Programme for Economic Expansion* (1959–64) were the first serious attempts at economic planning in Ireland. These also announced details of the future approach which would be pursued in relation to employment creation. The emphasis in the future was to be on export-oriented policies which attempted to attract foreign companies to Ireland and the abandonment of protectionism. One of the most important attractions was the Export Profits Tax Relief Scheme, whereby manufacturing firms were to be freed from taxation on profits earned on export sales. In addition to this, capital grants, re-equipment grants and loans at favourable rates of interest were made available to industries choosing Ireland as a location. These incentives proved to be a major attraction for foreign manufacturing firms – by the early 1970s overseas firms were responsible for over one-quarter of the total jobs in Irish manufacturing industry; by 1980 they accounted for one-third. Although indigenous manufacturing industry performed less well, total industrial and service employment both increased during the 1960s. As a result, the total number of non-agricultural jobs created during 1961–71 exceeded the number of jobs lost in agriculture – for the first time since the foundation of the state. The net increase in employment was modest at 2,300, but it was in stark contrast to the previous record. The increase in employment opportunities in Ireland accelerated during the 1970s. Between 1971 and 1979 a total of 97,000 net new jobs were created – about one-quarter of these being provided by multinational firms. Ireland became especially attractive for multinationals once Ireland joined the European Economic Community in 1973. Henceforth these firms had free access to the lucrative European market as well as attractive incentives provided by the Irish government. In any case, it was the jobs provided by these firms, as well as those created in the expanding services sector (both private and public) which influenced the substantial 'return migration' of the 1970s.

Despite the substantial net inflows, one must note the continuance of out-migration from Ireland in the younger age groups, even during the exceptional decade of the 1970s. Thus, Table 6.4 shows that the net loss in the 0–34 age groups amounted to over 60,000 persons during the decade in question. Data on 'one-year immigrants to the UK from Ireland' also confirm the persistence of gross outflows. In 1975 for example, these numbered 11,000; by 1983 they had increased to 17,500. These increases were accompanied by a dramatic drop in the number of 'one-year immigrants from the UK' – from 22,400 in 1975 to 8,800 in 1983.[14] The number of persons seeking assistance at the Irish Centre in London also points towards an increase in the numbers of Irish going to Britain in recent years. In 1982 only 744 people sought assistance at the Centre; in 1985 this number increased to 2,136.[15]

The continuance of emigration throughout the 1970s and 1980s should come as no surprise. Despite some successes, Ireland was not capable of providing sufficient jobs during these years for its expanding population and labour force. During the 1970s the labour force was growing at some 20,000 per annum; yet during this relatively successful period only about 12,000 net new jobs were being created. The Irish economy experienced increasing difficulties during the recession of the 1980s. Since the early 1960s job creation depended heavily on the growth of foreign-owned industries, but even those have showed signs of weakness in recent years.[16] The consequence was a significant increase in unemployment. In this respect, young people have been especially vulnerable – in 1975 there were 45,000 unemployed under twenty-five years of age; by 1983 this figure had increased to 75,000 i.e. 20 per cent of the labour force in that age group.[17] As we have seen earlier, this is the group most heavily represented in the recent migration outflows.

We are thus reminded that the basic cause of emigration remains unchanged, that is the absence of sufficient employment opportunities in Ireland. This link between emigration and employment has been emphasised in a variety of studies during the last decade.[18] These also point to an association between the level of emigration and the rate of unemployment in Britain, confirming the view that the two countries represent, in effect, one labour market. Reductions in employment opportunities in Ireland and the deterioration of the unemployment rate in Ireland relative to Britain thus appear to be crucial determinants of emigration. Because of the short distance between the two countries and the ease of access, Britain tends to be a first point of search for employment.

It now appears that the vast majority of current emigrants to Britain come from urban areas in Ireland, in stark contrast to the situation in the 1950s. Unlike the 1950s, the brunt of those entering Britain have skills, education and training. Many however are ill-prepared for some of the realities of emigration to Britain in the 1980s, including declining employment opportunities and homelessness.[19] Those planning to emigrate likewise face poor employment opportunities in other EEC countries and restrictions on permanent entry to the United States.

Before concluding, one might usefully ask whether emigration has always been an undesirable phenomenon? It could of course be argued that the exodus from Ireland was a normal 'adjustment' process, whereby surplus labour moved to areas in Britain where it was required and remunerated. Apart from the gains to the individual emigrant in terms of employment and increased income, it could also be suggested that the outflow need not represent a significant loss to Ireland. Thus, the Irish nation has gained in the past from emigrants' remittances and from expenditure on holiday visits. When 'return migration' occurred, at least some of those returning brought newly-acquired skills, initiative and experience.[20]

However, one can also identify a variety of costs accruing to Ireland as a result of emigration. Successive Irish governments since Independence have spent substantial sums on educating the population at all levels. The state has placed an enormous emphasis on the acquisition of skills and training, especially during the last few decades. The continuing exodus of those with such skills, training and education increases the productive capacity of the host country but represents a similar loss in productive capacity to the Irish state. In such a situation, the Irish tax-payer pays for the training and education of those who leave, but reaps few of the benefits. If the foregoing has any validity, then Britain has, in effect, been receiving a hidden subsidy from her poorer neighbour. The limited research to date on this topic certainly suggests that, as far as the Irish state is concerned, the costs of emigration are likely to be greater than the benefits.[21]

This chapter has shown that, apart from a brief period during the 1970s, emigration from Ireland continued on a substantial scale during every intercensal period since the foundation of the State. Until the 1930s the vast bulk of Irish emigrants had gone to the United States. Since then, however, increased employment opportunities and ease of access made Britain the favourite destination. There are signs that net emigration is again on the increase – during 1985–86 the official figure is estimated to be 31,000 (all destinations). Yet the emigrant today faces reduced job prospects in Britain and Europe as well as restrictions on permanent entry to the United States. These difficulties underline the need to resolve our economic problems without delay and to give urgent priority to the provision of sufficient and viable employment in Ireland.

Acknowledgement: I am most grateful to John Blackwell and Dermot McAleese for helpful comments on an earlier draft.

REFERENCES

1. David Fitzpatrick, *Irish Emigration, 1801–1921*, Studies in Irish Economic and Social History, No 1, (Dublin, 1984). See also Patrick Blessing, 'Irish emigration to the United States, 1800–1920', in P. J. Drudy (ed.), *The Irish in America: Emigration, Assimilation and Impact, Irish Studies, Vol. 4* (Cambridge, 1985).
2. Louis Cullen, *An Economic History of Ireland since 1660* (London, 1972). F. S. L. Lyons, *Ireland since the Famine* (London, 1971), chapter 2. For a useful survey of the various interpretations of Irish industrial decline see Eoin O'Malley, 'The decline of Irish industry in the nineteenth century', *Economic and Social Review*, Vol. 13, No 1, 1981, pp. 21–42.
3. It could be argued that Ireland's colonial past contributed to a status of 'dependency' which facilitated, and even encouraged, migration. Thus, Ireland, was dependent, both before and after Independence, in relation to trade, investment, administration and migration. For this viewpoint, see Dudley Seers, Bernard Schaffer and Marja-Liisa Kiljunen (eds), *Underdeveloped Europe: Studies in Core-Periphery Relations* (Sussex, 1979) especially Parts 1 and 4; James Wickham, 'Dependence and state structure: foreign firms and industrial policy in the Republic of Ireland', in Otmar Holl (ed.), *Small States in Europe and Dependence*, Austrian Institute for International Affairs, 1983, pp. 164–83.
4. For an excellent overview of this period, see John O'Hagan and K. McStay, *The Evolution of Manufacturing Industry in Ireland*, (Dublin, 1981).
5. For an elaboration on these points see P. J. Drudy (ed.) *Ireland: Land, Politics and People, Irish Studies Vol. 2* (Cambridge, 1982), pp. 191–216.
6. John A. Jackson, *The Irish in Britain* (London, 1963), pp. 28–9.
7. Commission on Emigration and Other Population Problems 1948–54, *Reports* Pr 2541, (Dublin, 1955), p. 135.
8. *Ibid.*, p. 125. This figure for Britain has been disputed and it has been argued convincingly to be closer to 20 per cent for the late nineteenth century. See Cormac Ó Gráda, 'A note on nineteenth-century emigration statistics', *Population Studies*, Vol. 29, No 1, 1975, pp. 143–49.
9. *Historical Statistics of the United States: Colonial Times to 1970* (Washington, 1975). See also P. J. Drudy (ed.), *The Irish in America, op. cit.*, Appendix Table 4.2.
10. William S. Bernard, 'Immigration: history of US policy', in S. Thernstrom (ed.) *Harvard Encyclopedia of American Ethnic*

Groups (Cambridge, Mass., 1980); P. J. Drudy (ed.) *The Irish in America, op cit.* (Cambridge, 1985), pp. 72–76.
11. Donal Garvey, 'The history of migration flows in the Republic of Ireland', *Population Trends*, Vol. 39, Spring 1985, pp. 22–30.
12. *ibid.*, p. 26.
13. F. X. Kirwan, 'Recent Anglo-Irish migration: the evidence of the British labour force surveys', *Economic and Social Review*, Vol. 13, No 2, 1982, pp. 191–203; F. X. Kirwan and A. G. Nairn, 'Migrant employment and the recession: the case of the Irish in Britain', *International Migration Review*, Vol. 17, No 4, 1983, pp. 672–81.
14. Data provided by the Central Statistics Office, Dublin.
15. *Annual Reports*, Irish Centre, London.
16. See Eoin O'Malley, 'Foreign-owned industry in Ireland: performance and prospects', in *Medium Term Outlook 1986–1990*, Economic and Social Research Institute (Dublin, 1986), pp. 45–53. For assessments of Irish industrial policy and recent government responses see, for example, NESC, *A Review of Industrial Policy*, Telesis Report (Dublin, 1982); Frances Ruane, 'Manufacturing industry' in J. O'Hagan (ed.), *The Irish Economy: Policy and Performance*, (Dublin, 1984), 4th edn; White Paper, *Industrial Policy* (Dublin, 1984); White Paper, *Building on Reality, 1985–7* (Dublin, 1984).
17. J. Sexton, *Recent Trends in Youth Unemployment*, Economic and Social Research Institute Policy Series, (Dublin, 1983), p. 6.
18. See, for example, Brendan Walsh, 'Expectations, information and human migration: specifying an econometric model of Irish migration to Britain', *Journal of Regional Science*, Vol. 14, 1974; J. G. Hughes and B. M. Walsh, 'Migration flows between Ireland, the United Kingdom and the Rest of the World', *European Demographic Information Bulletin*, Vol. 7, No 4, 1976; J. G. Keenan, 'Unemployment, emigration and the labour force', in B. R. Dowling and J. Durkan (eds), *Irish Economic Policy* (Dublin, 1978); Patrick Honohan, 'The evolution of the rate of unemployment in Ireland, 1962–1983', *Quarterly Economic Commentary*, May 1984; Dermot McAleese, 'Anglo-Irish economic interdependence: the effects of post-1979 changes in the British economy on Ireland', *Irish Banking Review*, Spring 1986, pp. 3–16.
19. Tom Connor, *Irish Youth in London: Research Report*, Action Group for Irish Youth, (London, 1985).
20. For a summary of these arguments see Brendan Walsh, 'Labour market strategies', in Dowling and Durkan, *op. cit.*, pp. 212–15; B. J. Whelan and J. G. Hughes, *A Survey of Returned and*

Intending Emigrants to Ireland, Economic and Social Research Institute (Dublin, 1976); C. Maguire and D. Murphy, *Research and Development in Ireland*, (Dublin, 1978).
21. See, for example, Cormac Ó Gráda, 'On two aspects of post-war Irish emigration', Discussion Paper Series No 52, Centre for Economic Policy Research, (London, 1985). See Richard Lynn, *The Irish Brain Drain*, Economic and Social Research Institute (Dublin, 1968) for the cost implications of graduate emigration during the 1960s.

7 · The Irish in Britain
JOHN A. JACKSON

Britain has been a major destination for Irish emigrants since well before the industrial revolution and Ireland has equally provided a labour reserve for the British economy. The short distance across the Irish Sea and the lack of formal controls on movement have facilitated a process that has deeply affected both islands. Although demographically these effects have been more striking in Ireland where emigration to Britain and the rest of the world contributed to a net loss of population between 1851 and 1961, in the same period the Irish have been numerically the most significant minority in Britain. Two waves are apparent in the flow of Irish migrants to Britain since census data on birthplace became available after 1841. The first associated with the Great Famine in Ireland rose to a peak in 1861 of some 602,000 in England and Wales and a further 204,000 in Scotland. The numbers of Irish-born then declined at each census until reaching a low in 1901 of 426,565 in England and Wales and 205,064 in Scotland. The second wave built up in the 1930s and the war years but is principally associated with the decade of the 1950s and led to a peak of 957,830 Irish-born (north and south) recorded in Britain in 1971.

In this chapter emphasis is placed on this second wave and on those born in the Irish Republic. It is not always possible to separate origins for the Irish-born since precise origins are not always given in census or other statistics, and some of the references to the Irish in Britain aggregate those born in Northern Ireland with those born in the Irish Republic. It is perhaps also important to point out that, as with other data, place of birth does not automatically denote a particular nationality or commitment on the part of the emigrants themselves.

In the 1921 Census 1.0 per cent of the population of England

and Wales was born in Ireland and 3.3 per cent of the population of Scotland. Something of a watershed had been reached between the nineteenth-century pattern and its stabilisation and the beginning of the build-up to the new wave in the middle years of the present century. The formation of the new state also coincided with increasing controls and the introduction of a quota system on migration to the United States. Thus, although many of the sentiments of nationalism might have turned the emigrant away from the neighbouring country, Britain remained the most accessible destination for Irish emigrants following Independence.

This trend is apparent in the 1931 figures for England and Wales even though the percentage of Irish-born in the population continued to fall. The depression in the early years of that decade even led to a net inflow to the Republic of Ireland for the two years 1931 and 1932.[1] The position in Scotland however needs to be distinguished since there, in contrast to England and Wales, the number of Irish-born has continued to decline both numerically and proportionately since reaching a proportional peak in 1851 when 7.2 per cent of the population were born in Ireland and a numerical peak in 1881 with 218,745 recorded.

There was no census in 1941 as a result of the Second World War, but by 1951 when the first post-war census was held the number of Irish-born in England and Wales had almost doubled confirming a new trend which was caused in part by war-time factors and the immediate post-war expansion of economic activity in Britain. Although the Irish Republic remained neutral, Britain was able to draw selectively on Irish labour during the war years and the records of the Ministry of Labour, which was responsible during that period for the issue of travel permits, suggest that between 1943 and 1945 40,229 men and 35,502 women were recruited in this way and in the period between 1946 and 1950 when the scheme ended, a further 66,075 men and 78,119 women were added to their number.[2] The 1951 Census indicated that the total Irish-born community in Britain amounted to some 716,000 people. The majority (72 per cent) were drawn from the Irish Republic and they were distributed predominantly in the larger urban areas of England and Wales, particularly in the London and South-East region and in the Midlands.

In an interesting analysis of the post-war distribution patterns of the Irish in Britain, Walter has shown that in the period up to 1951 of this second wave of heavy Irish immigration, the numbers of Irish-born corresponded closely with population increase.[3] However, in the period since 1951 the main areas to gain in numbers of Irish-born were the East- and West-Midlands rather than the rapidly expanding South-West and East-Anglian regions (see Table 7.1). Walter attributes this to a time-lag effect caused in part by the heavy and continued attraction of semi-skilled and unskilled manual occupations for the majority of the immigrants and at that time the relatively young age of the Irish population which meant that they did not contribute significantly to 'retirement' redistribution which in part accounts for the growth of population in East-Anglia and the South-West.

The 1951 population of the Irish-born in Britain can be characterised as predominantly urban with more than half recorded in the six conurbations of Greater London (202,638), West-Midlands (45,722), Merseyside (32,231), South-East Lancashire (43,288), West Yorkshire (16,719), and Tyneside (4,858). Within these large urban areas particularly heavy clusters of Irish-born persons were to be found in certain districts and it is these concentrations, concealed by the aggregate figures, that were most significant in the appearance of an explicit Irish presence in Britain and provided the basis for an Irish ethnic community. Within London, for instance, in 1951, 8.4 per cent of the population of Paddington was Irish-born, and more than 5 per cent of the boroughs of Chelsea, St Pancras, Westminster, Holborn, Hammersmith, Kensington and St Marylebone could be similarly classified.

It could also be said of the Irish in 1951 that they were a predominantly young population, typically single and predominantly female.[4] It is these demographic characteristics among the settlers up to 1951 and in the succeeding decade of

Table 7.1. *Rates of change, by region, of total population of Great Britain, Irish Republic-born and Northern Irish-born, 1931–71*

Region		Percentage change		
		GB	IR-born	NI-born
(a) 1931–51				
10–20%	West Midlands	+18.18	+270.18	+474.95
	South East	+13.31	+81.07	+99.52
	East Anglia	+12.00	+115.10	+414.94
	East Midlands	+11.61	+115.44	+209.44
0–10%	South West	+7.98	+32.29	+82.90
	Yorkshire Humber	+5.26	+29.57	+96.13
	Scotland	+5.23	−18.67	−36.15
	North West	+5.21	−9.00	+24.95
	North	+3.27	−13.29	−7.39
	Wales	+0.21	−7.93	+113.36
(b) 1951–71				
over 20%	South West	+24.84	+31.66	+98.35
	East Anglia	+20.70	+34.05	+106.96
10–20%	East Midlands	+16.30	+73.30	+102.62
	West Midlands	+15.38	+72.24	+65.38
	South East	+11.77	+52.46	+69.91
0–10%	Yorkshire Humber	+6.45	+32.48	+78.98
	North	+4.83	−0.34	+21.13
	Wales	+4.83	+1.73	+58.92
	North West	+4.37	+21.80	+41.46
	Scotland	+2.49	−21.63	−24.36

Source: Walter (1980) Ref. 3, p. 303, Table 11.

heavy immigration from Ireland that define in large measure the now aging Irish-born population to be found in Britain thirty years later.

Distribution of this population is the result both of the effect of direct migration from Ireland, which traditionally has been directed to the known centres of attraction such as London and Birmingham, supported by relatives and others already located and subsequent moves that have taken place within Britain. In her analysis of two samples of immigrants in two contrasting industrial towns, Bolton and Luton, Walter finds that about half of the respondents arrived directly from Ireland while the remainder had located there after one or more subsequent moves. Significantly, in both cases the direct migrants had come to the town principally because of a friend or relative already there, whereas the arrival of the indirect migrants was mostly the result of economic opportunities.[5]

The occupations in which the Irish were to be found in 1951 and the areas in which they settled were the results of a combination of traditional areas of recruitment and new areas opened up as a result of war-time recruitment. During the war, industries with no previous experience of Irish labour had drawn in workers from Ireland and considerable diversification took place. Thus, in the period of post-war construction employers continued to draw directly from the Irish labour pool. In 1946, for instance, when the Ministry of Labour scheme was still operating, some 2,200 coalminers were recruited from the Irish Republic as well as nurses, and workers in metal manufacture and agriculture.

The occupational diffusion of the Irish-born in Britain apparent in the 1951 Census data as a result of post-war recruitment and a rise in professionally qualified migrants is perhaps as striking as the spatial diffusion that we have noted above. This diffusion is evident despite the relative concentration among males in the three categories of Building, Metal Manufacture and Unskilled which account for 45 per cent of all employed Irish-born and any females in the Professions and Personal Service which accounts for 61 per cent of all employed Irish-born women. This dispersal remained evident in the results of the 1961 and 1971 Censuses. In the latter Census, the birthplace information shows those born in the Irish Republic to be both less economically active as the result of aging but also in a much wider pattern of economic activity.

Of the males born in the Irish Republic aged fifteen and over and resident in Britain in 1971, 10 per cent were economically inactive and the vast majority of those were

Table 7.2. *Occupational categories of Irish Republic-born in Britain in 1971 (percentages)*

		Male	Female
I	Professional	3.0	2.0
II	Intermediate	9.0	16.0
III	Skilled non-manual	7.0	15.0
IV	Skilled manual	34.0	23.0
V	Partly skilled manual	20.0	24.0
VI	Unskilled manual	20.0	11.0
VII	Unclassified	5.0	9.0
		100.0	100.0

Source: Office of Population and Censuses, 1971, *Country of Birth Supplement,* London, HMSO, 1978. It should be noted that 39 per cent of Irish Republic-born women in Britain are recorded as economically active. Rounding errors result in discrepancies in percentage totals. The equivalent figures for 1981 are not yet available. For Heads of Household information for 1981, see Table 7.3.

retired. Of those economically active, 10 per cent were unemployed and a further 11 per cent of those in employment were self-employed. The broad social group breakdown for that year is indicated in Table 7.2. This shows the extent to which the Irish, for both sexes, have resisted the tendency to simply accept the role of an underclass by taking the jobs the British workers did not want in the period since the Second World War. Instead they penetrated deeply into the occupational and social structure at all levels (see also Table 7.3).

Since the 1971 figures are the last available published data which give any details of the occupations of the Irish-born, it is useful also to consider the extent to which occupationally the Irish-born have contributed to that share of the labour market that is filled by the total immigrant population in Britain. In broad terms 25 per cent of male immigrants in employment and 29 per cent of female immigrants in employment in 1971 were drawn from the Irish Republic. These aggregate figures, however, fail to reveal the extent to which the Irish-born retain, even after the heavy Common-

Table 7.3. *Economic and industrial activity of heads of households born in the Irish Republic and resident in Britain, 1981*

Industrial category	Males (%)	Females (%)
Agriculture, Forestry and Fishing	1	0
Energy and Water Supply Industries	3	1
Mineral and Ore Extraction and Manufacture	4	2
Metal Goods Engineering and Vehicle Industries	15	7
Other Manufacturing Industries	8	9
Construction	26	2
Distribution, Hotels and Catering, Repairs	13	23
Transport and Communication	10	5
Banking, Finance and Insurance	6	13
Other Services	16	39
	100	100
	N = 23,934	N = 7,604

wealth immigration after the war, a dominant position within the overall immigrant community in certain sectors. Thus, of immigrant males employed in Construction, 64 per cent have a birthplace in the Irish Republic, 34 per cent of those in Vehicle Construction, and 42 per cent of those working in Gas and Water. These form significant enclaves within the labour market in sectors where the proportion of immigrant workers is already high. A somewhat similar, though less striking, situation is found in female occupations, where, for instance, those born in the Irish Republic represent 33 per cent of those immigrants employed in the Distributive Trades, 20 per cent of those employed in Insurance, Finance and Business and 29 per cent of those in Professional and Scientific Occupations.

The Irish-born community in Britain declined by over 100,000 during the period 1971–81 and almost 70,000 left Britain for Ireland during the same period.[6] As a result, the characteristics of the Irish in Britain have changed considerably. The economic depression and rising rates of unemployment in Britain combined with increased economic activity in the Irish Republic during that decade resulted in net in-migration to Ireland. Although there is evidence that net emigration from Ireland is increasing again in the mid-1980s, the scale of movement, at least to Britain, is slight compared to earlier periods. Thus, the aging Irish population of the 1940s and 1950s is not being fully replaced by new arrivals. In addition to those who have died or returned to Ireland to retire, the Irish population in Britain is increasingly less involved in direct economic activity. Whereas 18 per cent of the population of Britain is of pensionable age, 22 per cent of those born in the Irish Republic fall into this category; 59 per cent are over 45 years of age compared with 38 per cent for the general population. Similarly, whereas 22 per cent of the population of Britain was under fifteen in 1981, this was only the case for 1.7 per cent of the Irish population.[7] These various statistics based upon birth in the Irish Republic ignore the reality of a situation in which the children of those immigrants settled in Britain and born in Britain are excluded from definition as part of the Irish community. Once an attempt is made to assess the size of the subjectively perceived Irish community in Britain we leave the relative security of census data to attempt an assessment of less tangible factors with regard to the experience of the Irish in contemporary British society.

Not only is the Irish community in Britain older and more settled than it was in the 1950s, but it is also living in a changed situation in Britain itself. As a result of the Northern Ireland 'troubles' since 1969 and acts of terrorism associated with them, being Irish in Britain has a symbolic meaning today that was absent twenty-five years ago. This is not to say that the immigrant then did not experience the residual anti-Irish prejudice, the ignorance of Irish history, and the trained incapacity of the English to comprehend Irish reality found by immigrants at all periods. Fuelled in the eighteenth century by anti-Catholicism culminating in the Gordon Riots, in the nineteenth century by a Darwinism that gave the

Irish simian features in the pages of *Punch*, and in the twentieth with the Irish joke (universally anti-Irish), there has been ready material for the British to assert superiority against the immigrant 'invader'. More substantial accusations of blacklegging labour and undercutting wage rates, overcrowded housing and consequent disease, conviviality and rowdiness added fuel to the flames, allowing problems inherent in British society itself to be attributed to and blamed on the immigrant.[8]

The more striking contrast with the decade of the 1950s though is the presence in Britain today of a significant community of black immigrants from the Commonwealth whose presence has highlighted much of the latent prejudice of an increasingly disillusioned and uncertain imperial nation. The evident contradictions apparent in the development of legislation to control immigration during the 1960s and 1970s, particularly the 1962, 1968 and 1971 UK Immigration Acts, were all designed as restrictive measures particularly aimed at limiting entry to Britain of black Commonwealth citizens.

In general the situation of the Irish in Britain has been weakened by the development of immigration and security controls in Britain. Entry was largely uncontrolled until the 1960s and under the 1948 British Nationality Act the 'special position' of citizens of the Irish Republic was recognised. This entitled them to vote and to apply for naturalisation after five years' residence without other conditions. In the 1950s the Irish were also treated very much 'at parity' with British residents and Commonwealth citizens. They enjoyed voting rights at national and local elections, social security and freedom of movement without declaration to the police or immigration authorities. A degree of reciprocity and 'normalisation' had been achieved following the controls established during the war with extensive co-operation in the social security field and even in the courts where the practice on both sides of the Irish Sea tended toward 'binding over' in order to encourage the defendant to take the boat.[9]

While many aspects of these arrangements, which were the

underpinning of free labour movement, became subsumed under EEC provisions once both countries became members of the EEC, increasing ambiguity has developed as a result of restrictions on Commonwealth immigrants and attempts to control terrorism. As successive measures have been passed by the legislature, particularly those which give wide discretionary powers to immigration officers, Home Office officials and the police, it has become increasingly unclear where the Irish immigrant stands. The recent case of the psychiatrist Dr O'Shea illustrates the point well. Dr O'Shea, a sixty-six-year-old woman residing in Britain, was held in jail on suspicion for five weeks during 1985. In a trial some twelve months later, she was found 'not guilty' of any offence. The Irish are clearly vulnerable in a climate of suspicion to arrest and questioning, and being from Ireland is a sufficient reason to expect terrorist involvement such that a person is placed in the invidious position of having to prove innocence.

A second tendency has been observable in the running account of prejudice against the Irish within Britain. In a climate in which deeply-felt racial prejudice is suppressed by legislation some of the aggravation that is undoubtedly felt is directed toward the Irish as a target, legitimated by suspicions that have been reinforced by a poorly understood awareness of the situation in Northern Ireland and indeed in the Irish Republic itself.

The Irish in Britain, unlike the majority of the 'Gästarbeiter' who provided for the labour needs of West Germany, France, Holland or Switzerland after the Second World War, have full rights of social security and welfare, can vote and can stay as long as they wish without any specific controls. Thus they are not treated as aliens under the law. Consequently, many immigrants from Ireland have adapted and identified quickly and smoothly to the British communities in which they live and gradually lose, especially as their British-born children grow up, the ambition to return to Ireland except perhaps for retirement or holidays. We have seen earlier that significant numbers returned to Ireland during the exceptional decade of the 1970s.[10] The large majority, however, did not return and probably will not return even when they retire. They have reconciled the sense of longing celebrated in Irish emigrant ballads and the sense of loss and detachment of real identity caught so well in the Goon Show song 'I'm walking backwards for Christmas across the Irish Sea'. In a study of 111 Irish emigrants from Skibbereen in West Cork conducted in Britain in 1965, 62 per cent expressed a desire to return to Ireland but 27 per cent specifically claimed that they would not like to return. Of this admittedly small sample, some 54 per cent expected that they would live in Britain for the rest of their lives. Perhaps, more strikingly, 12 per cent considered themselves now more English than Irish and one-third claimed to have exclusively English friends.[11] This process of gradual adaptation should, however, be contrasted with the clear evidence of an Irish ethnic community captured in newspapers such as *The Irish Post* and in clubs and pubs, dance-halls and hurling matches in areas of Irish concentration such as Camden Town in London or Handsworth in Birmingham.

The formal institutions of the Irish immigrant community in Britain, its traditional support for the Catholic Church and the tendency to vote for the Labour Party remain to define the possibility of a distinctive Irish ethnic sub-set of British experience. Both the Church in Britain and the Labour Party have felt somewhat uncomfortable with the support that they have received and have been reluctant to become too closely identified with Irish interests and issues.[12] The clubs and pubs and an increasing involvement in local community politics however in the past thirty years have given the post-war immigrants tangible involvement in British society and a growing sense of a community identity which is not limited to the working class. In contrast to the County Associations that were the centre of activity in the 1950s, there is today an emerging but coherent ethnic identity among the Irish in Britain which is more comparable to that of the American-Irish. Such a community plays a dual role: it accepts its place in the host society – being Irish is a way of being American or British – but at the same time keeps an informed interest and preserved opinion regarding affairs in Ireland itself. The ethnic consciousness has been enhanced by the necessity for the Irish in Britain to compete at a local level with other ethnic groups with a greater objective identity and less opportunity to 'pass' than has been available to the Irish themselves.

As Walter has shown in the study referred to above, the 'length of immigration affects the mix of Irish-born and those of Irish descent, which influences attitudes to Irish people in the town'.[13] It also influences the attitudes of the Irish themselves. Unfortunately there has been little detailed study in recent years of the process of settlement by the Irish community in Britain. It is, however, generally agreed that the twin influences of the problem of Northern Ireland and its consequences and the increased significance of race relations in British cities in the last twenty years have served to polarise the Irish community and to force those who wish to assert an Irish identity to develop it within an Irish ethnic conclave.

This focus on the settlement process of the Irish in Britain should not detract from an awareness of the dynamics of the migration process itself. While there was a particularly heavy migration of young people from Ireland in the post-war period, emigration from Ireland has continued and today appears to be again increasing. The problems associated with young people arriving in Britain ill-prepared for life in an English city and without employment or accommodation still continue to justify the work of charities such as the Irish Centre in Camden Town.[14] Notably today the Irish government, which formerly did not like to be seen to do anything that would appear to encourage emigration, supports the Centre's activities with a small grant and there is much more awareness and more response to the situation of the emigrant within Ireland itself. Emigration may no longer be viewed as a response to desperation; rather it is considered more selectively and consciously than in the past. However, it remains a reality especially for many young people in the Irish Republic which has at present both the highest national unemployment rate and the youngest population in Europe.

This chapter has given a necessarily brief account of some features of the Irish-born population resident in Britain over the sixty years that have elapsed since the foundation of the Irish Free State in 1922. Those who came to Britain in the 1920s left an Ireland recovering from Civil War for a Britain yet to experience the mass unemployment of the 1930s, the Jarrow Marches and the Second World War. Those who are still alive, are now very old men and women. Those who travelled after them, together with the sons, daughters and grandchildren of these, all contribute to an Irish community that has a very mixed and varied relationship with the homeland. Some keep frequent and close contact through visits to family and friends; others have little use for an Irish past in an English, Welsh or Scottish present. In that sense it is impossible to capture or categorise the wealth and variety of experience and subjective interpretation that constitutes the reality of the Irish community in Britain. Equally, changes in Britain itself, particularly a reluctant admission of the existence of a highly pluralised society, gives a salience to the Irish identity as a way of belonging in Britain that has eluded many of the immigrants in the past. By definition, migrants from Ireland in Britain as well as British people living in Ireland experience and express the relationship between the two countries, the antagonism, the suspicion, the paradoxes, and equally the shared aspirations and hopes.

REFERENCES

1. J. A. Jackson, *The Irish in Britain* (London, 1963), Appendix, Table xii, p. 194.
2. Jackson, *The Irish in Britain*, Table xiv, p. 195.'
3. B. Walter, 'Time–space patterns of second-wave Irish immigration into British towns', *Transactions of the Institute of British Geographers*, New Series, Vol. 5, No 3, 1980, p. 313.
4. Jackson, *The Irish in Britain*, pp. 18–19.
5. Walter, 'Time–space patterns', p. 313. On this point, see also H. Lind, 'Internal migration in Britain', in J. A. Jackson (ed.), *Migration* (Cambridge, 1969).
6. D. Garvey, 'The history of migration flows in the Republic of Ireland', *Population Trends*, No 39, Spring 1985. In an important

recent contribution, Kirwan and Nairn analyse the effects of the economic recession in Britain on the employment of the Irish community. They attribute a part of the contraction in Irish male employment between 1971 and 1977 to the characteristic concentration of Irish workers in building, construction and allied industries hardest hit in a recessionary climate. F. X. Kirwan and A. G. Nairn, 'Migrant employment and the recession – the case of the Irish in Britain', *International Migration Review*, Vol. 17, No 4, 1983.
7. *Labour Force Survey*, HMSO (London, 1981).
8. For a detailed description of this background of attitudes, see Chapter 8 of Jackson, *The Irish in Britain*. See also J. A. Jackson 'The Irish in Britain', in *Minority Experience*, The Open University (Milton Keynes, 1982).
9. On this practice, see note 12 on pp. 183 and 184 of *The Irish in Britain*.
10. Garvey, 'The history of migration'. See also chapter 6 of this volume.
11. J. A. Jackson, *Report on the Skibbereen Social Survey* (Dublin, 1967), p. 39.
12. Again on this see Jackson, *The Irish in Britain* and an excellent general account by J. Walvin, *Passage to Britain* (London, 1984).
13. Walter, 'Time–space patterns', p. 314.
14. For a recent study of Irish young people and their needs in London, see Tom Connor, *Irish Youth in London Survey*, Action Group for Irish Youth (London, 1985).

8 · Unequal sovereigns: the diplomatic dimension of Anglo-Irish relations

PATRICK KEATINGE

'Anglo-Irish relations' has long been a label of convenience which confuses two distinctions, the first between nationalities and the second between geographical entities. Given the existence of a separate Irish state, officially called 'Ireland' but not coterminous with the island of the same name, this politically charged confusion possesses a diplomatic dimension. Two sovereigns exist where there was one, but their relationship has been marred by the residue of a long and bitter antagonism. In recent years, with the persistence of political violence in Northern Ireland, it has become a conventional wisdom in both capitals that the conflict there requires common action by the sovereign governments. Less self-evident, however, has been agreement on the extent, mode or feasibility of such action, while opposing views of its likely or desired outcomes reflect a political chasm as deep as that which existed sixty years ago.

This unbalanced and often uneasy bilateral relationship between Dublin and London has been the focus of increasing scholarly interest in recent years, with detailed historical investigations of the earlier period being supplemented by attempts to analyse the turbulent events since the late 1960s. The following survey of the main themes raised in these writings attempts first to provide an outline of the diplomatic connection itself and then briefly to indicate its effects on the Northern issue. The first objective raises three questions. In what general setting did the British and Irish governments attempt to define their relationship? What sorts of issues were at stake between them? With what administrative and political resources was policy made, and the diplomatic dimension of Anglo-Irish relations implemented? Different answers may be found in each of the three periods examined below, but so too are several constants, not least being the intractable problem of Northern Ireland.

INDEPENDENCE TO WORLD WAR

The formative years of the diplomatic relationship between Dublin and London coincided with one of the most revolutionary eras in modern international relations. The certainties of the nineteenth-century European balance of power had been shattered, but not yet replaced by the relative stability of the superpower rivalry between the United States and the Soviet Union. The absence of these two states from the centre of the diplomatic stage shifted the burden of creating and maintaining a new international order back on to the shoulders of those established European great powers which had failed so miserably in 1914. The adoption of a new institutional framework for settling interstate disputes, the League of Nations, could not long disguise the fact that neither the political map nor the distribution of power was agreed.

For British governments the dilemmas arising from this state of affairs were particularly acute. Although the United Kingdom's imperial domains had never been greater than at the end of the First World War an objective assessment suggested over-commitment rather than confident ascendancy; too many debts remained to be paid and the very diminution of the United Kingdom itself – with the creation of the Irish Free State in 1921–22 – was a harbinger of decline. British attempts to stave off decline, simply to hold what they already possessed, were reflected mainly in the apppeasement of those forces challenging the status quo, first in the context of the Empire being transformed into the Commonwealth, and later in the turmoil of Germany's revival.

The inter-war period was also one of considerable transition in British domestic politics. The composition of the first post-war government set the tone with a Liberal prime-minister, Lloyd George, a coalition primarily dependent on

Conservative support, and the Labour Party providing the long-term challenge. This important transition in party fortunes was played out against a backdrop of rapid social change and economic deterioration. But so far as Britain's position in the world was concerned there was one constant – the reluctance of the Conservative Party, and particularly its 'diehard' right-wing, to accept the underlying trend towards decline.

The position of the new Irish state was by any criterion weak. As with many of the new states created in the aftermath of the the First World War the principle of national self-determination had been easier to assert than to apply. Economic dependence on the United Kingdom was overwhelming and even the formal diplomatic independence of the state was at first qualified by the ambiguities entailed in the status of a Dominion in the new Commonwealth. Unquestionably a small state, with a population marked by persistent emigration, the Irish Free State's concerns were those of survival rather than world influence.

Yet the internal politics of the new state during its first two decades were based on the refusal of a large part of the Nationalist Movement to accept the limitations of the circumstances in which it found itself. The civil war of 1922–23 ensured that Irish party politics continued in a long-established mould where 'the great divide ... had always been between those who supported and those who opposed the British connection'.[1] Republican diehards in Ireland would attempt to force the pace of change in Anglo-Irish relations with as little reverence for objective realities as their Tory counterparts.

The central issue in Anglo-Irish relations for the greater part of this period was the definition of the constitutional relationship between the two states. For British governments it was essential that the Free State maintain a formal connection with the Crown, and up to the mid-1930s this requirement was the yardstick by which other issues were judged. Seen as the essence of the 1921 Treaty, should it be repudiated in any way it was argued that the Irish state would become, in

Churchill's words, 'an anomalous body without a status at all, either in or out of the empire'.² The implications of Ireland's status for the Empire–Commonwealth, however, outlasted this initial emphasis on British constitutional theory and practice, for as a European war seemed more likely and the support of the Dominions became more necessary, the basic concern was that Ireland should not serve as an example for other malingering Dominions. Canada, Australia and South Africa, although naturally prone to the temptations of isolationism, might not be easily motivated by the sort of anti-British sentiment found in Irish nationalism, but India was another matter, which often proved to be an important consideration in Britain's policy towards Ireland.

Irish governments approached the constitutional issue in reverse order. The Cumann na nGaedheal governments in the 1920s concentrated on defining Dominion status in the most permissive manner possible; with the active support of other Dominions and Britain's gradual acceptance of looser imperial ties the Irish government found its legal status significantly improved by the Statute of Westminster in 1931.³ It was only when Eamon De Valera came to power in 1932 that a frontal assault was mounted on the terms of the 1921 Treaty; legislation to abolish the oath of allegiance was followed by the re-defining of the link to the Crown through the formula of 'External Association' during the abdication crisis in 1936, and a year later a new Irish constitution was adopted.⁴ To all of these Irish initiatives, with but one exception, British governments acquiesced.

The exception to British acceptance of constitutional change was the reserve placed on Articles 2 and 3 of the 1937 Constitution, which claimed ultimate sovereignty over Northern Ireland. British policy on the partition of Ireland, implemented by the Government of Ireland Act in 1920, combined a modicum of wishful thinking about peaceful re-unification within the Empire with a determination not to coerce the newly established Unionist Provincial Government in Belfast. The promise, in the 1921 Treaty, of some degree of repartition through a boundary commission was a cynical improvisation given too much credence on the Irish side.⁵ Between 1925, when this became obvious, and 1938, when De Valera attempted to negotiate with London on the issue, there was no development beyond the consolidation of the Unionist regime. De Valera proved to be no more successful than his predecessors, either in formal negotiations in 1938 or in the extraordinary crisis after the fall of France in 1940, when in return for the end of Irish neutrality the British government made ambiguous noises about some future move on Irish unification.⁶

This crisis, 'Britain's worst strategic situation since Napoleon',⁷ was the most serious test to date of Anglo-Irish diplomacy. Britain's strategic interests in Ireland had been expressed in the 1921 Treaty, particularly in the retention of specified naval bases, a fact which in itself precluded Irish neutrality in a future war. However, the military value of these bases was always at issue between naval and army planners. They were conceded to the Irish government in the negotiations of 1938 and even under the pressures of war their reconquest was never calculated to be equal to the likely political or military costs.⁸

Irish strategic interests were even more ambiguous. It is difficult to escape the impression that the state's essential dependence for external security on the United Kingdom was quite readily accepted through a mixture of fatalism and reluctance to pay the price of a credible national defence. Even when the ports were returned, and neutrality became a technically feasible option rather than a loosely conceived aspiration, Irish defence preparations were tardy and in many respects rudimentary. Neutrality, however, acquired its significance not in terms of defence but rather as the ultimate proof of sovereignty, through pursuit of a foreign policy that was visibly independent of the United Kingdom's. With the entry into the war of the two future superpowers in 1941 the strategic issue in Anglo-Irish relations became less acute, and especially with the belligerence of the United States Irish neutrality became a function of partition as well as of sovereignty.⁹

Economic issues between Dublin and London were a less dramatic feature of the bilateral relationship – their most striking manifestation, the so-called Economic War in the mid-1930s, was a by-product of the constitutional dispute – but they attest to its essential asymmetry. The continuity of British commercial and financial interests was unbroken by political independence; by the same token Irish dependence on the United Kingdom was always very high. The Cumann na nGaedheal governments took the view that this mattered less than the need simply to prove that they had the capacity to govern within the terms of the *laissez-faire* orthodoxy of the 1920s. Their Fianna Fáil successors, on the other hand, had much more ambitious aims of self-sufficiency and a correspondingly more active policy of intervention. Nevertheless, by the time the Second World War imposed its own form of self-sufficiency Irish trade and financial structures were still overwhelmingly oriented towards the United Kingdom.[10]

Given the extensive preoccupations of a great power at bay, for British governments the Anglo-Irish relationship was but one problem on a crowded agenda, and rarely the most critical. In the large, complex and deeply-rooted bureaucratic maze of Whitehall it was not always easy to sustain a sharp focus on Irish issues. After a confusing transitional stage following the 1921 Treaty the Dominions Office became the principal ministry involved, but the concerns of other departments were less consistent and the Foreign Office was hardly disposed to view any dominion as a serious sovereign state. Ireland had influential friends in the official establishment, such as Sir Warren Fisher at the Treasury, but the interplay of personalities and party interests at the political level was the key to British policy.[11] The direction and pace of policy-making partly depended on the personal priorities of, for example, Malcolm MacDonald as Dominions Secretary, or whether Neville Chamberlain or Winston Churchill was premier, but whoever was the driving force two political imperatives persisted. The first was a determination 'to exorcise the Irish incubus which had haunted British politics so relentlessly for so long';[12] the second was the pivotal position of the Conservatives in party politics and their dogged resistence to political change. The effect was to induce an attitude of inattention to Irish affairs, whether centred on Dublin or Belfast.

The policy-making process in Dublin was a mirror-image of all this. Administratively, at least so far as external relations were concerned, everything had to be learned, with sketchy resources and rudimentary structures. Nevertheless, partly making a virtue out of necessity, it did prove possible to concentrate governmental attention on Anglo-Irish relations in a much more sustained way than in London. Particularly in the 1930s, when De Valera was both premier and foreign minister, backed up by a very small group of officials, the Irish government possessed an unusual degree of flexibility and coherence. This was required as much by the exigencies of domestic politics as by diplomacy, given the overwhelming electoral significance of progress in redefining the 1921 Treaty. In this respect the indirect strategy adopted in the 1920s paid far fewer electoral dividends than the more radical revisionism of the 1930s.

The major theme of the diplomatic relationship between Dublin and London during this period was the struggle by the former to gain access to and influence with the latter, in the face of benign inattention at best and often a measure of irritation or hostility. The mode of communication varied. Full-scale bilateral negotiations at the highest level proved to be chastening for the Irish in 1921, but more successful for both sides in 1938, when a personal rapport was established between the two premiers. Routine. bilateral contacts remained in a transitional stage for most of the period, often bearing the marks of improvisation. Irish governments were represented in London by a High Commissioner and J. W. Dulanty filled that office over a long period to considerable effect; yet he had no counterpart in Dublin until Sir John Maffey was accepted as British Representative to Ireland after the outbreak of the Second World War.

Multilateral networks were more than just a useful additional point of contact. Membership of the Commonwealth, however unpalatable to Irish nationalists, provided the opportunities and leverage which led to the Statute of Westminster. Participation in the League of Nations, which for the Irish also enhanced links with other Dominions, gave a measure of international recognition to the new Irish state which the British often still found hard to accept. Irish and British positions on the role of the League proved to be generally compatible, and De Valera's involvement with the Geneva organisation gave many opportunities for developing his personal diplomacy with British ministers. Yet the fact remains that after the Statute of Westminster in 1931 the most significant changes in the Anglo-Irish relationship, on the constitutional issue, were 'the result of unilateral decisions taken by Irish governments which British governments chose to ignore rather than resist'.[13]

For those forces which determined the outer limits of Anglo-Irish relations in the twenty years following the Treaty – diehard Conservatives on the one side and Republican nationalists on the other – the outcome was judged in terms of a 'zero-sum game', a conflict over an exclusive view of sovereignty where the winner takes all. By such a criterion both sides saw themselves as losers and nothing essential had changed.

This verdict obscures so much of what occurred in the period, and bears so little relevance to what can occur in a world of sovereign states, as to be a travesty. Irish statehood had been defined, implemented, re-defined and tested in time of war. In London, 'by the summer of 1941, a consensus had been arrived at which would govern British policy towards Ireland throughout the remainder of the war and for more than two decades thereafter'.[14] British governments had found it possible to live with the Irish state as a foreign country rather than as a 'restless dominion', though they would subsequently often be reluctant to pursue the logic of this discovery. What had not changed, however, nor shown any real sign of change, was the partition of the island, a constant of Anglo-Irish relations which was only more firmly entrenched during the Second World War.

DUBLIN AND LONDON IN THE 'PAX AMERICANA'

The quarter of a century following the Second World War, though marked by many great changes, was characterised by a constant element of stability – the bipolar rivalry between the new superpowers, the Soviet Union and the United States. The latter's predominance was perhaps the key to the unprecedented economic growth in the 'Western' group of countries, leading to an increasing optimism, even towards the East–West antagonism which appeared to be moderating in the move towards détente in the late 1960s.

The United Kingdom's adaptation to these new circumstances was not without trauma, involving as it did the final dissolution of imperial pretensions and a hesitant and frustrated vocation as just another 'medium power' in western Europe. Through these difficulties British governments attempted to maintain a minimum of self-respect by emphasising the notion of their 'special relationship' with the new hegemonic power, a relationship built on cultural affinity and a presumed need for tutelage. This view was held and promoted by the leadership of both political parties in what was now unequivocally a two-party system. It was a Labour government which actively advocated the North Atlantic Treaty, and, though a Conservative government had to bow the head in the Suez crisis of 1956, throughout this period the bipartisan consensus on the 'Atlantic' orientation of British foreign policy generally seemed immutable.

Ireland's accommodation to the post-war world was equally tentative. Until the 1960s economic dependence was thrown into greater relief by the failure to emulate developments elsewhere in western Europe; moreover the state's diplomatic persona remained shadowy prior to the delayed admission to the United Nations in 1955. Party politics had lost much of the sharp simplicity of its civil war origins without gaining an alternative focus until, in the late 1950s, the promotion of economic modernisation started to match the state with its external environment. However, tentative internationalisation remained the hallmark of Ireland's place in the world.

The principal issue between Dublin and London of the pre-war period – the constitutional question – appeared to make an early exit, with the formal declaration of a republic in 1949. On both sides this unilateral Irish initiative was accepted as the formalisation of a situation which had already existed for more than a decade. Even the simultaneous departure from the Commonwealth could be presented in the same light, given more flexible interpretations of the nature of Commonwealth membership and a more relaxed view in Whitehall towards the experience of Irish deviations within it.

This was but one reflection of the isolation in which Ireland now found itself following the successful maintenance of neutrality during the World War, for there was little place for neutrality in the new Pax Americana. The American minister in Dublin, David Gray, had already gone to some length to discredit the Irish stance in 1944 in order to keep the residue of the Irish question – partition – out of American domestic politics in the post-war era.[15] His spur was the memory of the Irish contribution to the American decision for isolationism in 1919, but in the Cold War such an outcome was less likely. When the Irish government declined to join NATO in 1949, on the stated grounds that partition precluded membership, the American response was one of indifference, while British interests were met by continued jurisdiction over Northern Ireland. The British political establishment felt indebted to the Unionist regime for its participation in the war and the Government's response to Dublin's positions on the Crown, the Commonwealth and the Atlantic Alliance had the effect of consolidating rather than eroding partition, in spite of considerable public agitation on the issue in the new Irish Republic.[16]

Following this early flurry of activity the partition issue was effectively abandoned to the IRA. Their border campaign of the mid-1950s inevitably caused tensions between Dublin and London, but had little lasting effect. Indeed, by 1965, against a background of benign neglect in London, Seán Lemass and Terence O'Neill appeared to be leading their respective polities towards a *de facto* rapprochement in which the rising tide of economic modernisation would in time engulf the remaining outcrops of atavistic nationalism.

The creation of NATO cast European security in a multilateral mould in which it became increasingly difficult to discern even the outlines of the specific strategic interests of Dublin and London. A British foothold in Northern Ireland may have been regarded as 'essential' in 1949,[17] but subsequent attitudes as yet remain for the most part buried in official archives. What is certain is that British involvement in NATO was henceforth oriented towards the commitment of force to the central front in Germany, and the requirements of home defence or a primarily maritime strategy were accordingly downrated; the particular place of Ireland in this scheme of things was therefore an unlikely public issue. Dublin governments, for their part, were faced with the problem of formulating a national defence policy in a world of nuclear alliances. While there is evidence of concern about this predicament at the governmental level (including a proposal for a bilateral alliance with the USA and ten years later a more flexible view of NATO),[18] it has never caused much anxiety among the public at large. So far as the defence of the state was concerned there was a reversion to the pre-war mood of fatalistic neglect. Economic issues, on the other hand, bore equally on Dublin and London, with the eventual emergence in 1961 of a common interest in joining the mainstream of European integration. British moves in this direction were delayed by a reluctance to abandon the role of leading a maritime post-imperial economic bloc, and by apprehensions concerning the extent and character of political commitment required by the original six members of what was to become the European Economic Community. Ireland's European vocation seemed at first to depend on the United Kingdom acquiring one, so extensive were the ties binding the two economies.[19] En route to the decision of 1961 Ireland had no interest in the British-led European Free Trade Area (EFTA), which excluded agriculture; after the failure of both states' applications to join the EEC in 1963, however, the Irish government's new commitment to industrial free trade found expression in the bilateral Anglo-Irish Free Trade Area (AIFTA) which started in 1966.

Once Dublin's initiatives of the late 1940s were absorbed, Irish affairs appeared to fall into a curious bureaucratic limbo in the British machinery of government. In spite of Ireland's departure from the Commonwealth, relations with Dublin were still largely channelled through the Commonwealth Office, which was not merged with the Foreign Office until 1968; this was a contributory factor to what has been called 'the Isle of Wight syndrome', a tendency 'to forget entirely that Ireland is independent'.[20] Much the same attitude was found at the political level, corresponding to a similar degree of inattention towards Northern Ireland. A small group of members of parliament with an interest in Ireland, mostly from the Labour Party, made little impression on general bipartisan neglect.

Dublin's administrative concentration on Anglo-Irish relations was also diverted. The Department of External Affairs became oriented towards the United Nations in 1955, while the shift of emphasis towards an economic foreign policy reduced its overall significance in the 1960s. The 'unfinished business' of partition remained an element in party politics but, particularly with the emergence in the early 1960s of the first post-independence generation of political and administrative leaders, it appeared more and more to be a matter of ritual. The *de facto* 'recognition' of the Unionist regime, symbolised by the Lemass–O'Neill meetings in 1965, was not the occasion for resignations from the Fianna Fáil cabinet.

The diplomatic traffic between the two capitals soon acquired a much more mundane character than either the previous or subsequent periods enjoyed. Intermittent ministerial contacts supplemented routine administrative links; there was little need or diplomatic opportunity for heads of government to meet formally 'at the summit'. What was perhaps not quite normal about this relationship was the persistent sensitivity about symbolising its legitimacy at the highest level; state visits would have to wait awhile.

Writing in the late 1950s an eminent American political scientist, Karl Deutsch, argued that the relationship between Ireland and the United Kingdom, like that between Canada and the United States, suggested a tendency away from the orthodoxies of interstate relations towards some form of integration.[21] Cultural, economic and social links seemed to reduce political antagonism in a bilateral system of 'complex interdependence';[22] economic modernisation over time would make Anglo-Irish relations a game without obvious winners and losers. This view was widely held in both Dublin and London up to 1969.

THE OLD PROBLEM IN A NEW EUROPE

The third period of Anglo-Irish diplomacy started with the visible erosion of political authority in Northern Ireland in 1969, and the efforts of the sovereign governments to adapt to this reality remain a central theme to this day. Instability and a reversion to pessimism and conflict were also striking features of the wider world, in which the new American hegemony was already showing signs of decline. The early 1970s saw the apotheosis of détente between the superpowers, but by the end of the decade the mood was one of new cold war. The United States abandoned its attempt to exert effective economic leadership in 1971, in the face of pressures which subsequently resulted in major recessions alleviated by occasional periods of growth.

For both British and Irish governments these uncertainties have been encountered within a common multilateral setting; membership of the European Economic Community again became a live issue in 1969 and was a reality by 1973. However, the significance of this regional vocation was seen in quite a different light in each capital. For London, 'Europe' was a contested issue; material gain appeared to be marginal and the terms of entry were subject to persistent re-definition. The 1970s also saw questions being raised about the political consensus achieved in the post-war period. A two-party system competing for a centrist vote was being challenged, first by demands for regional devolution and then an increasing polarisation between the major parties and the appearance of a third force, the Social Democratic-Alliance.

Membership of the European Economic Community made a more decisive impact in Dublin. Material advantages seemed clear-cut and membership involved a more sharply defined foreign policy role than that of the previous period.[23] Participation in a multilateral framework, in which the government had formal access to policy-making, implied a marked change from the previous situation where external blows were either met with fatalistic resignation or had to be countered within the unequal bilateral relationship with the United Kingdom. By the 1980s, however, the gloss was wearing off this optimism, as a combination of recession and electoral volatility served to change the language of political debate. From 1981 on the broad bipartisan consensus towards Irish foreign policy was to become noticeably patchy.

Since 1969 it has often seemed as if there were no other issue in Anglo-Irish relations than the conflict in Northern Ireland. However understandable this view, it detracts from the importance of the two states' differing interests within the European Economic Community.[24] For London the rationale for membership stressed potential opportunities for an ailing industrial economy, while for Dublin the main attraction was participation in the Community's already existing agricultural regime. Against a background of recession these orientations tended to appear more as alternatives than complements to each other, at least in the medium term – and governments usually operate in the medium term at best. Though the original package deal on entry favoured Ireland rather than the United Kingdom, by the 1980s the British approach, explicitly advocating budgetary stringency by the Community and implicitly relying on free market forces, was nearer the European orthodoxy.

British and Irish attitudes towards the political evolution of the Community have also differed. London has generally been dismissive of the long-term aspirations towards political union, which are still reflected in the stated policies of the original member-states; Dublin governments on the other hand have been more inclined to give them some credence, provided the condition of significant economic convergence is met.[25]

With regard to European Political Cooperation – the foreign policy consultations between member governments – there is also a rather different approach. British interests are much more extensive and substantial, in terms of both material and historical significance, than those of Ireland, and it is no surprise to find British positions reflecting the diplomatic traditions of a former great power as against the often 'moralist' stances of an unequivocally small state.[26] But given the EEC's failure to transcend national sovereignty as the basis of political authority, Anglo-Irish differences in any of the dimensions referred to are only to be expected, and since they are subsumed within a complex multilateral diplomatic framework they rarely put the two governments in a position of sustained and concentrated confrontation.

This is what has always been at risk, and sometimes realised, with regard to the persistent conflict in Northern Ireland. The initial major crisis in August 1969 was followed by more prolonged tension between the implementation of internment in August 1971 and direct rule in March 1972; the Loyalist strike in May 1974 and the hunger strikes of 1981 were further low points in a diplomatic relationship which could often expect to deal with the 'politics of the last atrocity' on a daily basis.[27]

Against this difficult background Dublin and London nevertheless found a common interest. The suppression, or at least containment, of political violence was its central element, Dublin governments feeling threatened by the potential IRA challenge to their legitimacy and London governments encountering the actual effects of violence within their jurisdiction. The search for a 'solution' or 'settlement' was bound to be more problematic, as the fate of the Sunningdale agreement of 1973 and the tortuous history of the 'inter-governmental process' in the 1980s showed only too clearly.

Neither sovereign government has felt itself able explicitly to repudiate the fundamentally opposed claims of its client community in Northern Ireland, even though both insist on non-violent expression of these positions and often behave as if the latters' incompatibility can be eliminated with the passage of time. Their dilemma is reflected in the distinction between 'internal' and 'inter-governmental' strategies, a formulation which has been less a clear intellectual basis for policy than a code which encapsulates conflicting goals. Giving greater priority to 'internal' reform, whether through power-sharing or direct rule, can be seen from Dublin as a denial of aspirations towards unification, whereas the 'inter-governmental' approach has been interpreted by unionists in Northern Ireland and Britain as a fatal weakening of London's sovereignty. Whatever the extent of special pleading in the advocacy of either position, both Dublin and London have found their policies to be highly constrained, the more so as the influence of moderate advocates, such as the SDLP or Official Unionists, is threatened by extremists who in the last resort set the political agenda. In this context the establishment of the Anglo-Irish Inter-governmental Conference, in the Hillsborough Agreement of November 1985, can be seen as an achievement for 'inter-governmentalism', but it is arguable that its success depends on internal reconciliation.[28]

The emphasis in the 1980s on the inter-governmental approach to Northern Ireland, combined with the deterioration of East-West relations, served to raise the question of the strategic dimension of Anglo-Irish relations, with the suggestion that Dublin was to abandon neutrality as a *quid pro quo* for unification. But in spite of strains within the Western Alliance British strategic interests have as yet maintained their orthodox continental orientation, while the perception of strategic interests in Dublin has remained as enigmatic as ever, though within the context of more explicit support for neutrality.[29] Indeed during the Falklands conflict in 1982 the latter was sufficiently strong to serve as a factor in one of the sharpest Anglo-Irish confrontations in recent years.[30]

That bilateral relations between Dublin and London have

not been more negatively affected by the Northern Ireland issue since 1969 may at least in part be ascribed to the fact that they exist within a broader diplomatic setting. As well as common membership of the European Community, an important third party in this respect has been the United States. The Irish-American card – so long the expected ace of Irish Nationalists but so often a disappointment, either because of American isolation or the prior claims of the Western Alliance – came back into the game during the 1970s. However its value has not been clear, for American administrations have found difficulty in controlling their own nationals' contributions to political violence in Northern Ireland, and neither British nor Irish governments can hope to retain the exclusive affection of Washington.[31]

One of the most striking features of the eruption of the Northern Ireland conflict in 1969 was the nakedness, both political and administrative, of the governments in both Dublin and London; both were badly informed and policies were formulated on an *ad hoc* basis. Since then the policy-making process has been transformed. In London a considerable degree of bureaucratic complexity has evolved. The two principal elements are the completely new Northern Ireland Office and the Foreign and Commonwealth Office, which is the channel to Dublin both for bilateral and many European issues; yet these form the tip of an iceberg composed of civil and military agencies at all levels of political authority, and coordinated with a high degree of formality, through the Cabinet Office.

Dublin has also experienced bureaucratic growth with the creation of a separate Anglo-Irish unit within the Department of Foreign Affairs and the increasing involvement of the Department of the Taoiseach, which in the 1980s came to acquire some of the characteristics of its British counterpart. But the fact remains that the relevant machinery of government in Dublin is on a significantly smaller scale than that in London, thereby allowing a greater degree of informality and flexibility, without being entirely free of bureaucratic jealousies.

On the political level the new visibility of Northern Ireland (literally, through constant television coverage) inevitably brought Anglo-Irish relations into the parliamentary arena. Although both the British Labour Party and the Liberals might espouse quite radical aims, such as a united Ireland, this was generally confined to an aspirational level in the context of party conferences; at Westminster there has been a persistent inter-party consensus supporting the much more cautious policies of the government of the day.

In Dublin a similar bipartisanship persisted during the 1970s, for the main disagreements over Northern policy occurred within Fianna Fáil, the government party at the time of the crisis of 1969. These were contained under the leadership of Jack Lynch, and even during the first government of his successor, Charles Haughey. From 1981, however, the latter's reversion to an explicitly maximalist position on the issue of unification marked the end of a serious bipartisanship in Dublin. The report of the New Ireland Forum in 1984, though signed by the leaders of all the main parties in the south as well as the northern SDLP, subsequently served to demonstrate rather than disguise the failure to arrive at an effective agreed position.

Whatever the outcome of the inter-governmental approach as a strategy, inter-governmental contacts between Dublin and London have been a much more significant fact of life during the last seventeen years than in either of the previous periods in Anglo-Irish diplomacy. The flow of business at official level has increased both in scope and intensity, with the relevant ambassadors being frequently involved on a day-to-day basis. Ministerial contacts have also increased quite markedly, both bilaterally and in the framework of the European Community. Above all, personal meetings between heads of government have become an accepted mode of diplomacy. Since 1975 European 'summits' have taken place three times a year, offering opportunities for bilateral discussions 'on the margins', and bilateral summits, a frequent though *ad hoc* feature during the 1970s, came closer to being formalised in the 1980s.

All of this is, to a considerable degree, only to be expected in the practice of diplomacy in the modern world; yet in so far as the Dublin–London axis is for both governments 'a special case',[32] it does illustrate the considerable resources that must be expended in order merely to start coming to grips with common problems. Moreover, for Dublin the problems of access to influence, and for London of inattention or neglect, are still significant considerations, in view of the overcharged agendas of modern governments. When the agenda contains an issue like Northern Ireland, where democratic political authority itself is at stake, it is hardly surprising if diplomacy on its own works no miracles.

'THE UNIQUE RELATIONSHIP'[33]

Looking at the whole experience of diplomatic relations between Dublin and London, the extent of change is appreciable. The international context has broadened from the tight disciplines of the post-imperial phase to the untidy jumble of opportunities and constraints characteristic of multilateral interdependence. In both capitals the task of creating and maintaining a welfare state transformed political debate and the role of government itself, with mixed consequences for both societies. The issues of Anglo-Irish relations have also changed. Anxieties over constitutional links receded; potential differences on strategic questions diffused with the establishment of durable military alliances in Europe. Economic transactions, much more prone to short-term fluctuations, came to the fore. In both Dublin and London, allowing for differences of scale, the era of 'big government' arrived, and the contacts between the two states necessarily involved a complex interplay between specifically bilateral matters and multilateral policy-making, in the European Community and beyond.

Nevertheless two constants are also evident. One, sometimes misjudged because it is so obvious, is the fundamental asymmetry of Anglo-Irish relations. The United Kingdom's greater size, based on population, territory, and the legacy of its nineteenth century primacy, must carry greater weight on critical issues in global or regional politics. No matter what variation there has been in the circumstances in which Irish governments have appealed for third party support *against* the policy of London, the effect of such appeals has depended on much broader considerations. Nowhere has this been more marked than in the role of the United States, at the same time the most promising source of external support for both governments. Thus, while in general Ireland has been able to compensate for many of the disadvantages of asymmetry, there are some clear limits to what is attainable through diplomatic activity.

One such limit, the second major constant emerging in this survey, is seen in the resistance to date of the partition issue to significant change by the sovereign governments. The occasions on which change was either sought or expected, or both, may have demonstrated bad faith, neglect and inadequate preparation and implementation of policy by one or both governments, but the common and arguably decisive element throughout has been the determination of Unionists in Northern Ireland not to participate in a united Irish state. It remains to be seen whether the fate of the latest attempt at a joint initiative, the Hillsborough Agreement of 1985, will prove to be any different from its predecessors. Undeniably the stakes are high; partition has had a corrosive effect on Anglo-Irish relations in that, through repeated statements of the opposed positions, the legitimacy of the relationship itself is called into question. It does not matter that the persistence of antagonistic rhetoric is primarily a function of inter- or intra-party politics; so long as it is deployed the diplomatic relationship is vulnerable and, far from producing decisive effects on partition, may be rendered sterile.

The historical experience of the relations between Dublin and London suggests, therefore, that the outstanding difficulty in the relationship – Northern Ireland – has to be seen in a much broader context than that of inter-governmental relations. This is not to deny the importance of attempting to find common ground between the capitals, but such an achievement in itself can hardly be seen as a sufficient condition for amelioration of the conflict in Northern Ireland.

REFERENCES

1. Ronan Fanning, *Independent Ireland* (Dublin, 1983), p. 42.
2. Cited in Paul Canning, *British Policy Towards Ireland 1921–1941* (Oxford, 1985), p. 129.
3. David Harkness, *The Restless Dominion* (London, 1969).
4. Deirdre McMahon, *Republicans and Imperialists: Anglo-Irish Relations in the 1930s* (New Haven, 1984); Canning, *British Policy*, chapter 8.
5. Canning, *British Policy*, chapters 4–7.
6. John Bowman, *De Valera and the Ulster Question 1917–1973* (Oxford, 1982); McMahon, *Republicans and Imperialists, op. cit.*
7. Canning, *British Policy*, p. 276.
8. Canning, *British Policy*, chapters 9, 12–14. The fullest account of the Irish experience of neutrality during the Second World War is Robert Fisk, *In Time of War: Ireland, Ulster and the Price of Neutrality 1939–45* (London, 1983). For a concise survey of Irish neutrality, see Patrick Keatinge, *A Singular Stance: Irish Neutrality in the 1980s* (Dublin, 1984), chapter 2.
9. Conor Cruise O'Brien, 'Ireland in international affairs', in Owen Dudley Edwards (ed.), *Conor Cruise O'Brien Introduces Ireland* (London, 1969).
10. Patrick Keatinge, *A Place Among the Nations: Issues of Irish Foreign Policy* (Dublin, 1978), chapter 7.
11. Canning, *British Policy*, p. 315.
12. Ronan Fanning, 'Anglo-Irish relations – partition and the British dimension in historical perspective', *Irish Studies in International Affairs,* Vol. 2, No 1, 1985, p. 14.
13. Fanning, 'Anglo-Irish relations', p. 15.
14. Canning, *British Policy*, p. 310.
15. T. Ryle Dwyer, *Irish Neutrality and the USA 1939–47.* (Dublin, 1977), chapters 9 and 10.
16. Ronan Fanning, 'The response of the London and Belfast governments to the declaration of the Republic of Ireland, 1948–49', *International Affairs*, Vol. 58, No 1 (1981–82); Raymond J. Raymond, 'Irish neutrality: ideology or pragmatism?' *International Affairs*, Vol. 60, No 1 (1983–84).
17. Cabinet Minutes of 12 January 1949, cited in Fanning, 'The response of the London and Belfast governments', p. 111.
18. Ronan Fanning, 'The United States and Irish participation in NATO: the debate of 1950', *Irish Studies in International Affairs*, Vol. 1, No 7, 1979.
19. Miriam Hederman, *The Road to Europe: Irish Attitudes 1948–61* (Dublin, 1983)
20. Sir John Peck, *Dublin from Downing Street* (Dublin, 1978), p. 18.

21. Karl W. Deutsch et al., *Political Community and the North Atlantic Area* (New York, 1957), p. 199.
22. For 'complex interdependence', see R. O. Keohane and J. S. Nye, *Power and Interdependence: World Politics in Transition* (Boston, 1977). On complex interdependence in Anglo-Irish relations, see Patrick Keatinge, 'An odd couple? Obstacles and opportunities in inter-state political cooperation between the Republic of Ireland and the United Kingdom', in Desmond Rea (ed.), *Political Cooperation in Divided Societies* (Dublin, 1982).
23. Patrick Keatinge, 'The Europeanisation of Irish foreign policy', in P. J. Drudy and Dermot McAleese (eds.), *Ireland and the European Community, Irish Studies*, Vol. 3 (Cambridge, 1984).
24. Eamonn Gallagher, 'Anglo-Irish relations in the European Community', *Irish Studies in International Affairs*, Vol. 2, No 1 November 1985; Drudy and McAleese (eds), *Ireland and the European Community*; David Coombes (ed.), *Ireland and the European Communities: Ten Years of Membership* (Dublin, 1983).
25. C. P. Fogarty, 'European union: implications for Ireland', Administration, Vol. 33, No 4, 1985.
26. Christopher Hill, 'Britain: a convenient schizophrenia', and Patrick Keatinge, 'Ireland: neutrality in EPC', in Christopher Hill (ed.), *National Foreign Policies and European Political Cooperation* (London, 1983).
27. Paul Arthur, 'Anglo-Irish relations and the Northern Ireland problem', *Irish Studies in International Affairs*, Vol. 2, No 1, 1985.
28. For the inter-governmental process, see the chapter by Paul Arthur in this book. Recent attempts to analyse the problem include Pádraig O'Malley, *The Uncivil Wars: Ireland Today* (Belfast, 1984); Kevin Boyle and Tom Hadden, *Ireland: a Positive Proposal* (Harmondsworth, 1985).
29. Keatinge, *A Singular Stance*, passim.
30. Norman MacQueen, 'The expedience of tradition: Ireland, international organisation and the Falklands crisis', *Political Studies*, Vol. 33, No 1, 1985.
31. Adrian Guelke, 'The American connection to the Northern Ireland conflict', *Irish Studies in International Affairs*, Vol. 1, No 4, 1984.
32. William Wallace, *Britain's Bilateral Links Within Western Europe* (London, 1984), p. 36.
33. This description of Anglo-Irish relations was employed in the communiqué following the summit meeting between Charles Haughey and Margaret Thatcher, 8 December 1980.

9 · Northern Ireland: the 'unfinished business' of Anglo-Irish relations

PAUL ARTHUR

When Eamon De Valera told Dominions Secretary, Malcolm MacDonald, in May 1938 that Anglo-Irish relations could never be settled so long as partition remained he was simply acknowledging that normal bilateral relations did not exist between Dublin and London because both claimed jurisdiction over a territory of indeterminate status. One says 'indeterminate' status although the juridicial position was clear – constitutionally the Northern Ireland government was subordinate in powers and status to Westminster. Difficulties arose because the subordinate legislature adapted over time the Government of Ireland Act (1920) to suit its own purposes. Thus it was not inaccurate to describe the Stormont system as 'a self-governing province with some of the trappings of sovereignty'.[1]

It has taken more than a decade of bitter communal violence and over two thousand deaths to persuade Dublin and London that a coordinated effort might staunch this bloodletting. They have attempted this through the Anglo-Irish process. To date there have been six summits – May and December 1980, November 1981, November 1983, November 1984 and November 1985 – ranging from the acceptance of the 'totality of relationships within these islands' (December 1980) through Mrs Thatcher's peremptory dismissal of the three preferred New Ireland Forum options of Irish unity, federation/confederation and joint authority (November 1984) to the signing of the Anglo-Irish Agreement at Hillsborough in November 1985. This last established – without derogation from the sovereignty of either government – an Inter-governmental Conference 'concerned with Northern Ireland and with relations between the two parts of the island of Ireland' to deal on a regular basis with political matters; security and related matters; legal matters, including the administration of justice; and the promotion of cross-border cooperation.

The Hillsborough Agreement may herald a new beginning in Anglo-Irish relations but it is conceivable that an accord, signed to encourage peace, reconciliation and stability, has the potential to destabilise the province fundamentally. The purpose of this chapter is to explain why the Northern Ireland problem has bedevilled Anglo-Irish relations. We are concerned with a multilateral issue involving political entities of varying statuses grappling with the perennial problems of political dialogue such as sovereignty and self-determination. At a more mundane level the relationship is concerned, at one remove, with a double minority problem which is affecting inter-state relations. In that respect, a recommendation of the Capatorti Report, prepared for the UN sub-commission on the Prevention of Discrimination and the Protection of Minorities (1969) is relevant: 'History shows that the minority problem can poison international relations .... When their rights are guaranteed and fully respected minority groups can serve as a link between States.' The Report goes on to recommend bilateral agreements dealing with minority rights 'based on mutual respect for the principles of the sovereignty and territorial integrity of the States concerned and non-interference in their internal affairs'.[2] Such a recommendation has uncanny relevance for contemporary Anglo-Irish negotiations.

SEARCHING FOR 'TERMS OF EQUALITY'

The real 'victor' of the Anglo-Irish settlements of 1920–22 was Britain. She had managed to quarantine the Irish question from domestic politics; she was to reduce Irish representation at Westminster from one-hundred-and-five MPs to forty-six and then to thirteen Ulster MPs; she was enabled to withdraw her troops and leave control with indigenous forces. Now she could get on with the real business of politics – after

1922, very little time was spent on Ulster affairs at Westminster. Nicholas Mansergh calculates it at one hour and fifty minutes in a period of just over a year in 1934–35, and Richard Rose estimated that the Commons devoted less than one-sixth of one per cent of its time to discussion of Northern Ireland questions between 1964–69.

The Government of Ireland Act was not viewed so benignly in Ireland. Ulster Unionists were entrusted with the daunting task of ensuring 'peace, order and good government' with limited financial resources, a hastily assembled defence force and an embittered and determined minority. The Constitution – the 1920 Act – did not seem especially formidable since its provisions 'were dictated with a view to political pacification rather than administrative efficiency'.[3] Devolved institutions in Belfast provided (in the sober words of the Kilbrandon Report, written some fifty years after partition) 'every inducement to the Government in London to keep Northern Ireland out of United Kingdom politics'.[4] A form of Anglo-Ulster relations emerged as Belfast re-negotiated its status within the United Kingdom in the years following partition. This did not constitute full-blown diplomatic relations, of course, but it did emphasise that Northern Ireland was 'a place apart' within the Kingdom. With the outbreak of civil war in the Irish Free state, London was no longer constrained to maintain Collins's credibility and, as a consequence, the Unionists were given a much freer hand to develop independent policies. A relationship of mutual accommodation prevailed between the sovereign power and the subordinate unit. Acquiring a large degree of security autonomy became a principal objective in Unionist strategy. The creation of the 'B' Specials increased Northern Ireland's viability which

> required not 'good' government but its own government, with as much administrative discretion as possible. Over the years, safeguarding this discretion was effectively to become Unionism's 'foreign policy'.[5]

One calculation puts Britain's contribution for the Specials in the period 1921–25 at £6.78m of a total cost of £7.5m. As early as March 1922 the Chancellor of the Exchequer in an effort to ward off a public row in the Commons about the Specials proposed that payments to them be included in an estimate making provision for unemployment and other services. Yet there were those who were alarmed about this security build-up: 'The British government has armed and is paying for forces which it is told by the one who controls them (i.e. Craig) will in certain eventualities be turned against itself'.[6]

Northern Ireland's viability was also threatened by the burdens of the financial restrictions of the 1920 Act, and in that respect, the 'history of Northern Ireland's financial relations with Great Britain has been one of evading the consequences of the Government of Ireland Act 1920'.[7] She was assisted in her evasion by London. First, there was the Colwyn Committee appointed to decide on what was a 'fair' contribution to the Imperial Exchequer (for services such as the armed forces, defence, the national debt and other items falling on the British exchequer). Colwyn undermined two of the major principles of the 1920 Act by providing a strong disincentive to the exercise of Northern Ireland's power to vary its own taxes, and by envisaging that the Imperial contribution might be reduced to vanishing point. A trend was set whereby Westminster's control over Stormont expenditure was minimised.

Payments to Northern Ireland ... were covered by permanent statutory authority. They were made out of the Consolidated Fund, and the annual approval of Parliament was not required. The only exception to this were agricultural payments.[8]

Gradually, Stormont built on these gains through the Unemployment Insurance Agreement (1926), Westminster's acceptance of the principles of parity (in 1938) and leeway (in 1944), and the Social Services Agreement (in 1948).

Much of the credit must go to the first Prime Minister, Sir James Craig. He set great store 'in his ability to advance Northern Ireland's interests by direct and personal contacts with imperial ministers ... Craig acted less at times as Northern Ireland's Prime Minister than as its ambassador in Britain'.[9] At home he built up a reputation as a profligate spender with electoral considerations in mind because he insisted that Westminster had a moral duty to bail the province out of any financial difficulties. This was not to the liking of the Treasury whose relations with Craig reached such a nadir that the latter was effectively excluded from financial negotiations between 1934–38. As for his successor, J. M. Andrews, the Treasury considered him 'a dangerous demagogue'.

Treasury animosity raises a more central issue. If Stormont was subordinate, to whom was she subordinate? There appears to have been no monolithic Westminster view about Northern Ireland. One Whitehall official drafted in after the imposition of direct rule described the local administration as a 'federation of baronies' – in other words frequent contact was established between officials on a department to department basis. There was no sustained generalist view and much depended on the exigencies of domestic politics and of British strategy. Thus, the Dominions Office, concerned with the wider imperial interests of international conciliation, was often hostile towards Stormont. But it was the Home Office which held ultimate authority. It acted as the official channel of communication between the governments of the United Kingdom and of Northern Ireland, ensuring that Northern Ireland's constitutional rights were not infringed and watching the province's interests generally. The arrangement suited Unionists admirably. There is ample evidence of Home Office hostility towards any anti-Unionist perspective in the 1930s, 1940s, 1950s, and 1960s. The arrangement is explained in the smug conclusion of the Permanent Under-Secretary for State in 1954:

Personal contacts which have been established between Home Office officials and their Northern Ireland colleagues have led to mutual understanding and goodwill in the handling of thorny problems, despite occasional difference of opinion.[10]

While reasonable relations could be expected with London, the same could not hold for Dublin. Here Northern Ireland sought equality of status. Her initial fears centred on the Boundary Commission and the creation of a Council of Ireland with a 'view to the eventual establishment of a

Parliament for the whole of Ireland'. Events were to suggest that Unionists need not have worried unduly and that both may have been cynical exercises to speed British withdrawal. Belfast was to absorb the Council of Ireland powers so that there was no longer any machinery, even in theory, for cross-border cooperation between governments other than the provision in the December 1925 agreement for the possibility of inter-governmental meetings on matters of common interest. They did not take place, although Section 1 of the Northern Ireland Act (1947) removed territorial restrictions to enable Stormont to legislate and enter into agreement with the Irish government concerning cross-border schemes for electricity, drainage and transport. All of this raises the (forgotten) Belfast–Dublin axis. We must remember that Ulster Unionism feared Irish unity as a form of economic impoverishment and cultural domination. With a history of mistrust for their (British) guarantors it was essential that they sought equality of status with their southern neighbours.

THE BELFAST–DUBLIN AXIS

Craig and Collins held two meetings in London in January and March 1922 concentrating on the Boundary Commission, on the Council of Ireland, and on the removal of an economic boycott by Dublin in return for Craig's undertaking to facilitate the return of Catholic workers to the Belfast shipyard. Here were all the ingredients of North-South conflict – charges of discrimination, concern with economic problems and fundamental difficulties over status. The last proved intractable. Craig had suggested that the Council of Ireland be replaced by joint meetings of both cabinets and that 'in all matters under the purview of the Council' each government consult each other 'on terms of equality'. Cosgrave countered with a proposal for a meeting of all Irish representatives (to involve the Catholic minority in the North), and he feared that 'terms of equality' would ensure a Loyalist veto. In any case, the outbreak of civil war led to a fundamental reappraisal of Northern policy, not least of which was a remarkable memorandum prepared by Ernest Blythe. He argued for 'recognition of the Northern government and implies that we shall influence all those within the Six Counties who look to us for guidance to acknowledge its authority and refrain from any attempt to prevent it working . . .'. Fanning describes this as 'the embryo of the non-violent constitutional Northern policy pursued by the successive governments of independent Ireland until the present day'.[11]

In fact, independent Ireland was caught in the horns of a dilemma. It could not offer formal recognition – nor, indeed, a conciliatory policy – because to do so was to raise the grave liability of admitting the separateness of the Loyalist community and thereby encourage a heightening of its claims. It did not have the military superiority to conquer the North, and, besides, the minority could be held as hostages. Instead it indulged in a constitutional hypocrisy – enshrined in Article 2 and 3 of the 1937 Constitution (Bunreacht na hÉireann) – which John Bowman describes more sensitively as 'aspirational' rather than 'operational'.[12] This was evident as early as 1924 when the Sinn Féin Member of Parliament for Fermanagh and Tyrone, Cahir Healy, wondered whether he should refuse to take his seat in order to help on the boundary issue. He was advised 'not to take his seat at present but not to do anything which would prejudice him in regard to taking his seat in future'.[13] Thirty years later De Valera summarised (implicity all Irish governments') objections to admitting Northern Nationalists to Dáil Éireann – they would be talking to the converted on the partition issue; they would have representation without taxation on other issues; and their presence in the Dáil might not be in the national interest since they might take sides between the Dáil parties.[14] It was to be another thirty years before a proper Northern influence made itself felt in Dublin with the Social Democratic and Labour Party (SDLP) participation in the New Ireland Forum.

In the intervening years Irish governments could do little but act as ombudsman for Northern Nationalist grievances but it could not convert concern into influence. Northern policy concentrated initially on the majority population through, as we have seen, a policy of non-recognition and passive resistance (including economic boycott). In 1927 De Valera made no secret of his approval of economic coercion; 'Let them feel what separation means . . . if Ulster chooses to remain outside our political system she can have no special right of access to our markets'.[15] Cross-border trade fell significantly between 1924–36. The simple fact was that, after 1925, Dublin did not believe that the Anglo-Irish quarrel was to be settled 'through a prior agreement with a Unionist *minority*' (to borrow De Valera's expression in 1921) but that it 'must be sought in the larger general play of English interests'.[16] Belfast became blurred in Dublin's vision as the latter strove for greater independence. Ironically, the more independence Ireland attained the wider the partitionist divide, and the longer partition 'held' the less interest displayed by London unless a crisis erupted. This has rightly been dubbed 'crisis management'. The 1937 Constitution, the 1938 Anglo-Irish agreements, neutrality during the Second World War, the Republic of Ireland Act (1948) led to Anglo-Irish relations being conducted in terms of absolute theoretical equality between two sovereign states, but at the price of increasing British sympathy for the Unionist cause. Fanning summarises the result:

But in 1948–49, as in 1921–22 and throughout the years between, the achievement of sovereignty took precedence over the aspiration of unity in the minds of those who controlled the destiny of independent Ireland.[17]

This exclusivist mentality was matched by Ulster Unionists who were vigilant in protecting their own interests. In the light of a Labour victory in 1945 some Unionists began to give serious consideration to greater independence through Dominion status, but the idea was extinct by the end of 1947 if only because to 'attempt a fundamental change in our constitutional position is to re-open the whole Irish question' (Sir Basil Brooke).[18] By 1952 Brooke, the Prime Minister, was writing to Churchill to express his bitter disappointment that

Britain had decided to call the South, 'The Republic of Ireland' and not 'The Irish Republic'. He almost succeeded in having the official name of Northern Ireland changed to 'Ulster'.[19] By the late 1950s we can speak confidently of the existence of 'two solitudes' in Ireland. Anglo-Irish relations were virtually non-existent. Contact between Belfast and Dublin was cursory and truculent. Little could be done for the Nationalist minority other than act as its megaphone. Besides, Nationalist pressure was neither coherent nor united.

A sea-change occurred with the appointment of Seán Lemass as Taoiseach in 1959. He extended the Taoiseach's role in the field of foreign affairs. His philosophy is encapsulated in a statement to the Dáil on 3 June 1959 that 'the historic task of this generation is to secure the economic foundation of independence'. He brought to a close the era of protectionism with its Sinn Féin concept of economic nationalism and self-sufficiency with the signing of the Anglo-Irish Free Trade Agreement in 1965. His economic nationalism was meant 'to confound those Northern defenders of partition who contend that in joining us in freedom would be an economic disadvantage to the north-eastern counties'.[20] His policies appeared to bear fruit in the years 1960–73 with a growth in Irish productivity of 9.1 per cent as compared with the United Kingdom of only 5.5 per cent. He displayed flexibility in the matter of Irish neutrality and he discouraged the constant use of the United Nations for anti-partitionist rhetoric. Politically, the culmination of his policy was the historic meeting at Stormont with Terence O'Neill in January 1965. It symbolised the end of the cold war in Ireland but it failed to give full legitimation to the O'Neill regime. He was a victim of strident loyalism and his downfall introduced a curious asymmetry into majority/minority relations inside Northern Ireland involving self-confident Nationalists and divided and demoralised Unionists. It was to be some time before this became self-evident.

THE TWO GUARANTORS

Dublin and London reacted in characteristic fashion when political violence again became part of the political agenda. Jack Lynch's response was verbal Republicanism and then (mostly) symbolic such as moving field hospitals to the border. Britain retaliated with the Downing Street declaration (August 1969) which affirmed 'that responsibility for affairs in Northern Ireland is entirely a matter of domestic consideration'. A lack of coordination was to be a feature of policy-making over the next decade as they reacted to the politics of the last atrocity and their deep mistrust of each other. In addition, they were engaged in attempting to control their own clients. William Craig, for example, resigned from the Northern Ireland government because he challenged Westminster's right to interfere in the province's affairs. Northern Ireland's Constitution was 'more than a mere act of Parliament', he declared, it represented an 'agreed settlement' – 'the settlement made when our grandfathers and fathers made their historic stand'.[21]

Dublin was uncertain who to turn to for advice in Northern Ireland. Nationalist politics were going through a trauma as a new leadership emerged from the civil rights campaign. Some – notably the Belfast socialists, Paddy Devlin and Gerry Fitt – mistrusted Fianna Fáil. Others were engaged in more dubious practices with the re-emergence of the IRA, and eventually three Fianna Fáil ministers left government accused of gun-running on behalf of Republicans. In reality, there was little that the Irish government could do. United Nations assistance was invoked on 20 August 1969 when Patrick Hillery, Minister for Foreign Affairs, requested, by virtue of Article 35 of the Charter 'an urgent meeting of the Security Council in connection with the situation in the Six Counties of Northern Ireland' – the partitionist language was redolent of emotional times. The general demeanour of Hillery, of Con Cremin, Ireland's Permanent Representative, and of Lord Caradon, the British representative, suggest that on this occasion catharsis was what mattered – the

United Nations as 'sacred drama'. In practice she was reduced to pursuing a policy of 'quiet diplomacy and personal conversation' (the Taoiseach's address to the United Nations, 22 October 1970) and acting as a spokesman for the minority through its role of 'second guarantor'. The latter was not always welcome to all factions of the SDLP which was concerned to demonstrate that its acquiesence in any agreement was essential. Equally 'quiet diplomacy' could not always be maintained – between August 1969 and early 1972 there were claims that there had been forty-seven cross-border incursions and twenty-seven over-flights by the British. Mr Lynch warned the Dáil (22 October 1971) that 'if there are repeated and more serious incursions by the British Army across the border it may be necessary to seize the United Nations of this issue as a threat to international peace'. Two months earlier, the *Daily Telegraph* (31 August) suggested that Anglo-Irish war is 'an ultimate possibility which cannot be logically excluded'.

The Unionist community presented even greater problems for Westminster. The former lacked political sophistication and leadership and placed too much reliance on a security response. The Troubles, too, led to intra-ethnic conflict so that a tripartite split in the Loyalist community made it difficult for policy-makers to know with whom to negotiate. Their one astute leader, Brian Faulkner, showed a willingness to move by holding out the prospect of a new Council of Ireland modelled on the 1920 Act. But it was as unattractive in 1971 as it had been in 1921 ... in fact, more so; the Home Secretary, Reginald Maudling, was speaking candidly in September 1971 of 'an active, permanent and guaranteed' role for both communities.

The imposition of Direct Rule in March 1972 removed all vestiges of power from the majority community. It provoked William Craig's Vanguard Unionists into asserting that the Ulster Loyalists are 'an old and historic community' for whom union with Britain had never been 'an end in itself', but 'was always a means of preserving Ulster's British tradition and the identity of her Loyalist people'. British politicians, 'by dismantling Ulster's capacity for resistance to friend (*sic*) or foe' had 'unwittingly forged a nation that cannot entrust to them its security or national destiny'.²² Since 1972 the Protestant majority community has explored fitfully its sense of identity. It has not yet accepted a distinctive Ulster 'nation' (perhaps because it cannot embrace so secular a doctrine). In place of a national consciousness it has developed a 'sense of ethnic honour, that is "of the excellence of one's own customs and the inferiority of alien ones"'.²³ As in the past it has relied on its own ethnic solidarity in time of crisis to pull it through. It has developed a variety of modes of reaction. Rhetoric: 'As long as (Ulster people) have a majority, even if the House wanted to put them into the Republic, it could not be done', Mr Paisley told Parliament in July 1980. Institutional resistance: Mr Paisley has urged the acceptance of the Northern Ireland as a 'bulwark for the Union'. Direct action; the 1974 Ulster Worker's Council strike, the 1977 'constitutional stoppage', a 'Third Force' in 1981. Beneath it all the fundamental dilemma remains – integrationist or devolutionist?; Loyalist (owing allegiance to 'Ulster') or Unionist (maintaining loyalty for the United Kingdom)?

More importantly, wittingly or not, direct rule has shifted strategy from internal to inter-governmental, and a Loyalist veto has become more difficult to impose. The Northern Ireland Office is not simply another territorial ministry. Unlike the Welsh and Scottish Office, all political options remain open, and the Secretary of State is immersed in political and security matters to an extent unimagined by his counterparts. For these reasons the Taoiseach welcomed the imposition of Direct Rule as a 'positive step' because it meant 'a recognition that it was not possible to work through existing structures'.

Since 1972 the two governments have worked in (not always harmonious) relations to fashion a solution. Patrick Keatinge has rightly described it as 'fever-chart diplomacy'. Human rights issues – allegations of torture against internees – have damaged relations between them from December 1971 and January 1978 when the European Court finally found against Britain for 'degrading and inhuman treatment'. When the Labour government found itself vulnerable to Unionist pressure between 1976–79, the Secretary of State, Roy Mason, was reluctant to discuss matters of cross-border cooperation with Dublin. Finally, the Falklands campaign induced deep divisions on the issue of supporting economic sanctions. Mr Haughey's explanation, that as a neutral country Ireland could support diplomatic pressure but not military activity, was not enough to satisfy the Unionist Member of Parliament, John Taylor:

> The Dublin government assumes that world reaction to Argentine would be the same to the Republic if it invaded Ulster – hence the desire of the Dublin government to help secure the acceptance of Argentinian forces in the Falklands and to dissuade the UK government from any worthwhile military response.'[24]

(A contingency plan drawn up for the Irish government in the mid-1970s suggested that its Army might have the capacity to capture the border town of Newry.) From an Irish perspective the impact of the hunger-strike in 1980–81 and the Government's failure to dissuade James Prior from pursuing his rolling devolution scheme in 1982, all diminished the Anglo-Irish process.

It needs to be recognised that both states' ultimate loyalties are to their own 'settled' domains so that domestic consideration could interfere with the inter-governmental process. Thus, Charles Haughey as Taoiseach and as Leader of the Opposition; in this manifestation he told the 1981 Fianna Fáil Ard-Fheis that a solution would require 'restraint and patience, understanding and generosity, and maybe a longer rather than a shorter period of time'. He demonstrated few of these qualities himself in the aftermath of the Hillsborough Agreement. And his Minister for Foreign Affairs chose to inflate the success of the December 1980 summit at a time of pressing economic problems for his government. Of course, it might be argued that Mr Haughey's adversarial disposition has the merit of protecting the Northern minority since the Anglo-Irish process is built on an ambiguous concept.

THE IRISH DIMENSION

The concept has been in vogue since October 1972, and before 1980 enjoyed only one short period of institutionalisation in the power-sharing period. The Council of Ireland was to have a ministerial tier charged with 'executive and harmonising' functions in such non-contentious areas as agriculture, electricity, tourism and transport. Any one individual – there were seven ministers each from the Irish government and the Northern Ireland Executive – had the power of veto. As a further inducement to Unionism Dublin 'solemnly declared that there could be no change in the status of Northern Ireland until a majority of the people of Northern Ireland desired a change in that status'. The dimension, then, was based on the constitutional guarantee. Secondly, it stressed functional cooperation. Thirdly, we should never under-estimate its anti-terrorism aspirations. Such were its limitations that David Miller could write of its creator, William Whitelaw:

> he demonstrated that he had learned an important lesson about Irish nationalism; that most of its adherents are much more concerned with symbols than with substance. The Council ... represented almost exactly what most Catholics, North and South, really wanted. It would legitimate an 'aspiration' to a United Ireland without actually threatening the higher standard of living enjoyed by northern Catholics by virtue of United Kingdom membership and without saddling southern Catholics with the unwanted burden of actually governing the troubled province over which their hearts and their constitution claimed jurisdiction.[25]

Symbols were important for the Loyalist community as well. The Irish dimension represents their symbol of encroaching Irish unity.[26]

With the collapse of power-sharing and its successor, the Constitutional Convention, policy-making settled into damage limitation, that is until Margaret Thatcher became Prime Minister in 1979. In her first newspaper interview she told the *New York Times* correspondent (12 November 1979) that she would not permit the 'squabbling political parties' in the province block her (then limited) political initiative. It was to be known as the Atkins initiative, and like its successor, the rolling devolution scheme, it floundered on the conflicting demands of the indigenous politicians. It is in this context, the failure of internal initiatives, that Anglo-Irish relations has proceeded.

Some general tendencies need to be noted. More regular contact at official and political level is producing greater trust in the inter-governmental process. The phrase 'in good faith' kept recurring in the joint Hillsborough press conference. It has led to a more solid relationship through the creation of new institutions – an Inter-governmental Council in 1981 and an Inter-governmental Conference serviced by a permanent Secretariat in 1985 – and a recognition of shared responsibility – 'the totality of relationships within these islands'. All of this has encouraged cooperative efforts on security and human rights issues and in cross-border social and economic cooperation.

A second theme has been the growing influence of the SDLP. It is the first constitutional Nationalist party to play a pivotal role in Belfast–Dublin *and* Belfast–London relations. This has arisen through stressing the wider dimensions of the problem. Its document, *Towards A New Ireland* (1972),[27] advocated a British declaration to withdraw from Northern Ireland pending Irish unity: in the interim a power-sharing government could be established and Northern Ireland would be a condominium under the joint sovereignty of the British and Irish governments. Nothing so radical has come to pass but given its lack of political power save for five months in 1974, its influence has remained durable and remarkable. In more recent years it has been of a more salutary kind as a barrier to Sinn Féin resurgence (denoted by the widespread acceptance that Catholic 'alienation' is a major factor in the equation). Of greatest significance is John Hume's persuasive power in getting the New Ireland Forum under way. In retrospect the Forum Report must be read as an agenda rather than a blueprint, and as an agenda central to Anglo-Irish negotiation. 'The most important aspect of the report is not the three options', Hume told the Commons on 2 July 1984, 'but the views of Irish

Nationalists about the ways in which realities must be faced if there is to be a solution'.

A final theme has been the disarray of the Loyalist parties. Their siege mentality has produced unanimity in declaring what they are against, but their positive qualities have been rather more lacking. Their sense of hurt and despair runs deep: 'We are going to be delivered, bound and trussed like a turkey ready for the oven, from one nation to another nation', Jim Molyneaux told the Northern Ireland Assembly on the day after the signing of the Hillsborough Agreement. The future of the Anglo-Irish process centres largely on this community as to whether it accepts willingly, with others, its subordinate status or whether we shall be forced towards the 'dreary steeples of Fermanagh and Tyrone' again. As matters now stand the new asymmetry in Anglo-Irish relations involves self-confident Catholics and demoralised and divided Unionists.

REFERENCES

1. I. Budge and C. O'Leary, *Belfast: Approach to Crisis. A Study of Belfast Politics, 1613–1970* (London, 1973), p. 143.
2. Cited in K. Boyle and T. Hadden, *Ireland. A Positive Proposal* (London, 1985) p. 47.
3. N. Mansergh, *The Government of Northern Ireland. A Study in Devolution* (London, 1936), p. 314.
4. *Royal Commission on the Constitution 1969–1973*, Cmnd 5460, (October 1973), para 1303 (The Kilbrandon Report).
5. P. Bew, P. Gibbon and H. Patterson, *The State in Northern Ireland* (Manchester, 1979), p. 62.
6. Bew, Gibbon and Patterson, *op. cit.*, fn. 3, p. 222.
7. Martin Wallace, *Northern Ireland: 50 Years of Self-Government* (Newton Abbot, 1971), p. 157.
8. Kilbrandon, *op. cit.*, paras 1272–1314.
9. P. Buckland, *The Factory of Grievances* (Dublin, 1979), p. 45.
10. Sir Frank Newsam, *The Home Office* (London, 1955), p. 172.
11. Ronan Fanning, *Independent Ireland* (Helicon, 1983), p. 35.
12. John Bowman, *De Valera and the Ulster Question 1917–73*, (Oxford, 1982), pp. 108–9.
13. Fanning, *Independent Ireland*, p. 89.
14. Bowman, *De Valera and the Ulster Question*, p. 284.

15. Bowman, *op. cit.*, p. 99.
16. Bowman, *op. cit.*, p. 16.
17. Fanning, *Independent Ireland*, p. 180.
18. Bew, Gibbon and Patterson, *op. cit.*, p. 123.
19. *The Irish Times*, 5 January 1983.
20. Cited in Susan Baker, 'Nationalist ideology and the industrial policy of Fianna Fáil (1955–72): the evidence of *The Irish Press*', in P. Arthur and M. Laver (eds), *Irish Political Studies* (PSAI Press, forthcoming).
21. David Miller, *Queen's Rebels*, (Dublin, 1978), p. 123.
22. Miller, *Queen's Rebels*, pp. 153–4.
23. R. Wallis, S. Bruce and D. Taylor, '"No surrender!" Paisleyism and the politics of ethnic identity', (Dept of Social Studies, Queen's University Belfast, 1986), p. 3 and passim.
24. *Belfast Telegraph*, 24 May 1982.
25. Miller, *Queen's Rebels*, pp. 159–60.
26. P. Arthur, 'Anglo-Irish relations and the Northern Ireland problem', *Irish Studies in International Affairs*, Vol. 2, No 1, 1985, pp. 37–50.
27. Social Democratic and Labour Party, *Towards a New Ireland* (Belfast, 1972).

Index

Aaron, H., 73
Abdication Crisis, 33, 142
Act of Union (1801), 2–6
  effects of, 13, 19
  Nationalist attitudes to, 7–9
  Protestant attitudes to, 9
  Repeal movement, 8
administration, Irish, 24, 45–62
  British in, 51–2
  changes in, 60–1
  contacts with Britain, 61
  financial system, 53–4
  hand-over, 49, 50–1, 58–9, 145
  see also civil service; Dublin Castle
agriculture
  dependence on Britain, 16, 22, 92–5
  and EEC, 97–8, 101, 104
  Free Trade Agreement, 96–7
  population loss, 110, 111–12
  protectionism, 90, 91, 93
  social welfare, 69–70
  structure of, 111–112
America see United States of America
Anderson, Sir John, 51–2
Andrews, J. M., 165
Anglo-Irish agreements, 16, 92
  Free Trade Agreement, 1965, 79, 96–7, 150, 169
  see also Treaty, 1921
Australia, 142

'B Specials', 163–4
Barry, Tom, 47
Beveridge Report, 65, 74, 76, 77
Bewley, T. K., 56
Blind Pension Act, 68
Blythe, Ernest, 17, 98, 167
  and Irish language, 60–1
Boland, H. P., 60
boundary commission, 143, 165–6
Bowman, John, 167
Brennan, Joe, 52, 53–4, 56, 58–9, 61
Briggs, A., 73

Britain
  Commonwealth immigrants, 130–1, 133
  economy of, 16–17, 87–105, 144 see also Economic War
  Empire, loss of 140, 147, 149
  and EEC, 22, 42, 81, 96, 114–15, 134, 149–55 passim
  and EMS, 99, 101
  Irish firms in, 93
  Irish immigrants, 22, 39, 107–15 passim, 118–20, 125–37
  community, 135–7
  control of entry, 133–4
  demography of, 127–8, 131–2
  distribution, 127–9
  occupations of, 129–31
  prejudice against, 132–4
  security of, 3, 4, 143
  unemployment in, 69, 73–4, 102–3, 117, 119
  and USA, 147
  welfare state, 73–8, 82–3
British Nationality Act, 1948, 133
Brooke, Sir Basil, 168–9
Bunreacht na hÉireann, 21, 29, 32–41
  amendments, 40–43
  Catholicism in, 36–7, 41–2
  compromises, 34
  and the EEC, 42–3
  financial system in, 53–4, 60, 142, 168
  Irish language in, 37
  Northern Ireland in, 35–7, 40, 167
Butt, Isaac, 89

Cabinet Office (British), 155
cabinet government, 26, 32, 59–60
Canada, 142, 151
Capatorti Report, 162
Capital Investment Advisory Committee, 117
Caradon, Lord, 170
Cavan, county, 110
censorship, 15

census data (British), 125–6, 129, 130–2
Chamberlain, Neville, 144
Chamberlain Act, 1925, 70
children's allowances, 81
Chubb, Basil, 60
Churchill, Winston, 45, 142, 144, 168
civil service (Irish)
  hand-over period, 49, 51–5
  ministerial accountability, 48–9
  organisation of, 56–9, 61
  pensions, 71
  recruitment, 71
  see also administration
Civil Service Commission, 56–7
Civil Service Regulations Act, 57
Civil War, 29, 50, 111, 141, 163, 166–7
Collins, Michael, 50, 52–3, 56, 57, 163, 166
  and Department of Finance, 48, 53, 55, 57
  and Irish language, 60
Colwyn Committee, 164
Common Agricultural Policy, 101
Commonwealth, British,
  immigrants from, 130–1, 133
  Irish Free State in, 27–9, 32–5, 38, 141–2, 145–6, 148
Commonwealth Office, 150
Congested Districts Board, 7
Conservative Party, 141, 145, 147
constitutional development, 22–43, 141–2
  Irish Constitution, 1919, 22, 25–6, 46
  Irish Constitution, 1922, 22, 27–32, 53–4, 59–60, 142
  Irish Constitution, 1937, *see* Bunreacht na hÉireann
Control of Manufactures Acts, 91, 93, 95
Conway, Cardinal, 42
Cosgrave, W. T., 56–62 *passim*, 166
Costello, John A., 38, 76
Council of Ireland, 165–6, 174
courts
  and EEC, 42
Craig, Sir James, 164–6
Craig, William, 170, 171
Cremin, Con, 170
culture,
  British influence on Irish, 8–9
  cultural nationalism, 13–15, 17–18
Cumann na nGaedheal, 32, 36, 144

Dáil Éireann,
  and administration, 48–58

First Dáil (1919), 25–6, 46–7
Provisional Government (1922), 27–32
Unionists in, 167
see also Parliament
Daly, Dr Mary, 91
Davis, Thomas, 12
De Valera, Eamon, 16, 17, 31, 49, 56, 61–2
  and Bunreacht na hÉireann, 26, 32–41, 60, 142
  and Economic War, 92
  as Foreign Minister, 145
  and League of Nations, 146
  and partition issue, 29, 33, 35–9, 143, 161, 167, 168
  and social policy, 69, 71–2, 76–7
de-colonisation, 18–19
dependency, 110–111
Deutsch, Karl, 151
Devlin, Paddy, 170
Dignan, Bishop John, 75–6
diplomatic relations, 139–58
  1922–39, 140–6
  1945–69, 147–61
  and Northern Ireland, 151–57
  asymmetry of, 157–8
divorce issue, 41, 42
dominion status, 141–2, 168
Dominions Office, 144, 165
Donegal, county, 112
Downing Street Declaration, 170
Dublin, 6, 8, 24
  parliament in, 2–5
  population rise, 108–10
Dublin Castle, 24, 50, 51–3
Dulanty, J. W., 145

Easter Rising, 1916, 8, 25, 34, 52
Economic Development 1958, 95, 117
Economic Expansion, First Programme for, 95, 117
economy (Irish)
  and Britain, 13, 87–105, 144
  integration with, 13, 23, 87–9
  after independence, 110–12 *see also* Economic War
  economic nationalism, 16–19, 94–5
  see also protectionism
  foreign investment, 97, 101, 117–18
  British investment, 96–7, 102
  industry, 41, 90–1 *see also* agriculture
Economic War, 59, 90–1, 93, 104, 111, 144
education system (Irish), 7, 8, 11, 24

Éire
  use of term, 34, 35
emigration (Irish)
  to Britain, 107–20 passim, 125–37
  costs and benefits of, 119–20
  after the Famine, 8, 9, 11, 66, 107
  after Second World War, 94, 108
  to USA, 107, 108, 112–14, 119–20
  see also return migration
Emigration, Commission on, 112
employment, 112, 115, 117–120, 129–131
European Convention of Human Rights, 42
European Court, 172–3
European Economic Community (EEC), 96, 149, 151
  and Britain, 22, 42, 81, 96, 114–15, 134, 149–55 passim
  entry negotiations, 96–7, 149
  and Ireland, 42, 81, 87, 98–101, 118, 134
  agriculture, 16, 17
  Constitution, 22, 41, 42–3
  and Northern Ireland, 104, 152–3, 155–6
European Free Trade Area (EFTA), 149
European Monetary System (EMS), 98–101
European Political Cooperation, 153
exchange controls, 100–1
Executive Authority (External Relations) Act, 1936, 35, 38
Export Profits Tax Relief Scheme, 95, 117
External Affairs, Department of, 150
'external association' policy, 34–5, 39, 142

Falklands conflict, 154, 173
Family Income Supplement, 80–1
Fanning, Ronan, 104, 167, 168
Farrell, Brian, 26, 47
Faulkner, Brian, 171
Fenians, 15
Ferguson, Sir Samuel, 13–14
Fianna Fáil, 32, 36, 40, 59, 61
  and Northern Ireland, 156, 170
  and protectionism, 15, 16, 89–94, 144
  and social policy, 69, 71–2, 76–7, 79
Finance, Department of, 48–9, 51, 57–8, 104
  British influence on, 54–5, 61
  powers of, 53–4
Fisher, Sir Warren, 51, 104, 144

Fitt, Gerry, 170
Ford Motor Company, 93
Foreign Affairs, Department of, 155
Foreign and Commonwealth Office, 155
Foreign Office, 144, 150
Fowler, Norman, 82
France, 4, 5, 143

Gaelic Athletic Association (GAA), 15
Gaelic League, 15
Gallagher, Eamonn, 104
Galway, county, 112
Garvey, Donal, 116
George, David Lloyd, 53, 140
Gladstone, W. E., 12
Glynn Committee, 70–1
government, Irish, 30, 145, 155
  British legacy, 45–62
  cabinet system, 26, 32, 48, 59–60
  parliamentary procedure, 46, 47
  terminology, 26, 55
  see also administration
Government of Ireland Act 1920, 27, 45, 52, 142, 161
  and Northern Ireland, 163, 164
Grattan, Henry, 89
Gray, David, 148
Great Famine, 7, 8, 9, 11, 66, 107, 125
Greenwood, Sir Hamar, 56
Gregg, C. J., 56
Griffith, Arthur, 47
Guinness, brewery, 93

Haughey, Charles, 156, 173
Healy, Cahir, 167
Hillery, Patrick, 170
Hillsborough Agreement 1985, 40, 154, 158, 161–2, 173–6 passim
Hogan, Patrick, 54
Home Office, 165
Home Rule movement, 8, 11–12, 45, 89
Hume, John, 175–6
hunger-strikes, 153, 173
Hyde, Douglas, 12, 14–15

Immigration Act 1924 (USA), 114
Immigration Acts (Britain), 133
Immigration and Nationality Act 1965 (USA), 114
India, 142
industry, Irish, 41, 90–1
Insurance (Intermittent Employment) Act 1942, 71–2
Inter-governmental Conference, 154,

161–2, 175
International Labour Organisation
  (ILO), 81
International Social Security
  Association, 81
Inter-Party government, 38, 76
internment, 153, 172–3
Ireland
  and Britain, 1, 22–3
  17th–18th c., 2–5
  Act of Union, 5–12
  to 1922, 12–20
  British living in, 107, 116
  defence policy, 143, 149 see also
    neutrality
  international role, 146, 147, 148–9
  politics in, 24, 28–32, 33, 50–1, 141,
    147
Ireland Act 1949, 39, 115
Irish–Ireland movement, 15
Irish Centre, London, 118, 136
Irish language, 8, 14–15, 17, 37, 60–1
Irish Republican Army (IRA), 29–30,
  34, 45, 50
  British military influence, 46–7
  and partition issue, 148–9, 153, 170

Jacobs Ltd, 93
Johnson, Tom, 30–1

Keatinge, Patrick, 172
Kennedy, Dr Henry, 56–7
Kennedy, Hugh, 28
Keynes, J. M., 90
Kilbrandon Report, 163
Kildare, county, 110

Labour Party (British), 141, 147
  and Ireland, 150, 156, 168, 173
  Irish support for, 135
  and social policy, 65, 75, 77–8
Labour Party (Irish), 30–1
land, 2, 7, 9 see also agriculture
Land Acts, 7, 9
land annuities, 90, 92
League of Nations, 140, 146
Leitrim, county, 110, 112
Lemass, Seán, 79, 148–9, 150, 169
Liberal Party, 140, 156
List, Friederich, 88
local government, 10, 24, 71
Louth, county, 110
Lynch, Jack, 156, 170–1
Lynch, Patrick, 94–5

MacBride, Seán, 61
MacDonald, Malcolm, 144, 161
McElligott, Jimmy, 51, 52–3
McGilligan, Patrick, 53
McGrath, George, 48
MacNeill, Eoin, 17, 47, 57
Maffey, Sir John, 145
Mansergh, Nicholas, 163
Mason, Roy, 173
Maudling, Reginald, 171
Mayo, county, 110, 112
means testing, 71, 78, 80–1
Meath, county, 110
media, influence of, 18, 41, 68, 133
Miller, David, 174
Molyneaux, James, 176
Monaghan, county, 110
monarch
  constitutional position, 27, 28, 33, 35
monetary systems, 87, 98–101, 103
Moran, D. P., 15
Mother and Child Scheme, 76
Murray, Dr C. H., 99, 100

National Health Insurance Society, 72,
  75
National Health Service (British), 75
national insurance, 67, 68, 73
nationalism, Irish, 12, 29
  and Act of Union, 7–9, 13, 19
  colonial, 3
  cultural, 13–19, 22, 23
  economic, 16–19, 94–5 see also
    protectionism
  and religion, 3–4, 11, 12, 23, 31
  vision of, 15–16, 19, 24–5
neutrality, 61, 111, 126, 143, 148, 154,
  168–9
New Ireland Forum, 156, 161, 167,
  175–6
North Atlantic Treaty Organisation
  (NATO), 147, 148, 149
Northern Ireland, 1, 2, 52, 89
  and Britain, 101, 132–4, 139, 142–3,
    146, 148–57 passim
  direct rule, 153, 171–2
  emigration from, 113, 116, 125
  and EEC, 104, 152–3, 155–6
  future of, 161–76
  and Irish culture, 14, 166
  and Irish Free State, 27
  and Irish Republic, 165–73
    Irish Dimension, 174–6 see also
      Hillsborough Agreement
    Nationalists in, 154–5, 166–9, 175

rolling devolution, 173, 175
Stormont administration, 163–5
Sunningdale Agreement, 153, 174
Unionists, 2, 10–11, 14, 28, 142, 150, 154, 158, 165–71 *passim*, 175 *see also* partition issue
Northern Ireland Act 1947, 166
Northern Ireland Office, 155, 172

O'Brien, Conor Cruise, 37
Ó Ceallaigh, Sean T., 17
Ó Cofaigh, Tomás, 101
O'Connell, Daniel, 5, 8, 9, 10
O'Connor Committee, 71
O'Hegarty, P. S., 55
O'Higgins, Kevin, 50
O'Neill, Captain Terence, 148–9, 150, 169
O'Shea, Dr Máire, 134
Occupational Injuries Scheme, 79, 82
Official Secrets Act, 57
Official Unionist Party, 154
old age pensions, 67, 68, 70–1, 73
Organisation for Economic Cooperation and Development (OECD), 81

Paisley, Rev Ian, 172
Parliament, British, 5–6, 45, 162
  model for Irish Constitution, 26, 30–1, 45, 47–8
Parliament, Irish, 2, 3, 5
Parnell, C. S., 9, 12
partition issue, 1, 29, 33–43 *passim*, 142–3, 146, 150
  cross-border trade, 168
  IRA border campaign, 148–9
Pearse, Patrick, 15
Pitt, William, 5
plantations, 2, 23
Plunkett, Horace, 13
police force, 7
Poor Law, 65–9, 73, 74
population, Irish, 107–10, 112, 115–16
Prior, James, 173
Progressive Democrats, 83
protectionism, 15, 16, 89–94, 102, 111, 117, 169
proportional representation, 28, 30
Protestants,
  and Act of Union, 5, 9–10, 11
  in administration, 51–2
  ascendancy, 2, 23
  nationalists, 3–4, 12
Public Assistance Act 1939, 71, 80

Quota Act 1921 (USA), 114

Redmon, Owen J., 59
Redundancy Payment Acts, 79–80
Republic of Ireland Act 1948, 38, 40, 168
return migration, 108, 116–18, 132, 134–5
Rimlinger, Gaston, 72
Rising 1916 *see* Easter Rising
rolling devolution, 173, 175
Roscommon, county, 110
Rose, Richard, 163

Scotland, 4, 14, 23, 49, 125, 126
Scott, Sir Walter, 14
secularisation, 41
Sinn Féin, 12, 15, 16, 29–30, 61, 175
  absention, 45
  and Constitution, 22, 25, 34
  and protectionism, 89, 94, 169
Sligo, county, 112
Social Democratic and Labour Party (SDLP), 154, 156, 167, 175–6
social policy, Irish,
  British legacy, 65–83
    after independence, 68–71
  Catholic influence, 36, 75–7
  development of, 41, 72–4, 78–81
  earnings-related benefit, 77–8, 80, 82–3
  and EEC, 81
  proportion of GNP, 73, 77, 78
  retrenchment, 82–3
  White Paper on, 76
Social Services Agreement 1948, 164
Social Welfare Act 1952, 76–7, 78
Social Welfare Commission, 83
socialism, 31, 66
South Africa, 142
Statute of Westminster 1931, 142, 146
Sunningdale Agreement, 153, 174
Supplementary Benefit Scheme, 78
Supplement Welfare Allowance Act 1975, 80

Taoiseach, Department of the, 155
Taylor, Sir John, 51
Taylor, John, 173
Thatcher, Margaret, 82, 161, 174
Tone, Theobald Wolfe, 12
trade, Irish, 13, 16–17, 87, 94–7, 111
  less dependent on Britain, 97–8, 101–2
  cross-border, 168

see also protectionism
trade union movement, 66, 68, 80
Treasury Department,
 and Ireland, 61, 104, 144
 and Northern Ireland, 165
 powers of, 49, 54, 55
Treaty of 1921, 27–8, 32, 52, 141–3, 145
Treaty of Rome, 42, 43

Ulster Workers' Council, 172
unemployment, 69, 73–4, 118–19, 136
 in Britain, 102–3, 117, 119, 132
Unemployment Act 1934, 69
Unemployment Assistance Act 1934, 69
Unemployment Insurance Agreement 1926, 164
Unionists, 2, 10–11, 14, 28, 51–2, 142, 150, 154, 158, 165–71 *passim*, 175
United Irishmen, 4
United Kingdom, *see* Britain
United Nations, 147, 150, 162, 169, 170–1
United States of America (USA), 3, 4, 26, 47, 92, 143, 147, 151
 emigration to, 107–8, 112–14, 119–120, 126, 135
 investment in Ireland, 97, 101
 and partition issue, 148, 155, 158

Vanguard Unionists, 171

Wales, 14, 23, 125–7
Walsh, Brendan, 98
Walsh, J. J., 56–7
Walter, B., 136
Wet Time Act, 71–2, 83
White Papers
 Economic Development, 95, 117
 Social Security, 76
Whitelaw, William, 174
Whyte, John, 31
widows' pensions, 70–1
Workmens' Compensation schemes, 67, 68, 73, 75, 78–9
World War (Second), 92–3, 111, 143

Yeats, W. B., 12
Young Ireland Movement, 15